REENGINEERING
REVISITED

Bala V. Balachandran
J.L. Kellogg Graduate School of Management
Northwestern University

S. Ramu Thiagarajan
Mellon Capital Management Corporation

A publication of Financial Executives Research Foundation, Inc.

Financial Executives Research Foundation, Inc.
10 Madison Avenue
P.O. Box 1938
Morristown, NJ 07962-1938
(973) 898-4608

International Standard Book Number 1-885065-16-7
Library of Congress Catalog Card Number 99-73811
Printed in the United States of America

First Printing

Financial Executives Research Foundation, Inc. (FERF®) is the research affiliate of Financial Executives Institute. The basic purpose of the Foundation is to sponsor research and publish informative material in the field of business management, with particular emphasis on the practice of financial management and its evolving role in the management of business.

The views set forth in this publication are those of the authors and do not necessarily represent those of the FERF Board as a whole, individual trustees, or the members of the Advisory Committee.

FERF publications can be ordered by calling 1-800-680-FERF
(U.S. and Canada only; international orders, please call 770-751-1986).
Quantity discounts are available.

ADVISORY COMMITTEE

Camille A. Guérin (Chairman)
Secretary-Treasurer (retired)
Canada Council for the Arts

John B. Kirby
Vice President, IBM Year 2000 Initiatives
IBM Corporation

J. James Lewis
Executive Vice President
Financial Executives Research Foundation, Inc.

William M. Sinnett
Project Manager
Financial Executives Research Foundation, Inc.

Norman E. Thompson
Senior Vice President
Strategic Enablement Services Finance
American Express Company

Rhona L. Ferling
Publications Manager
Financial Executives Research Foundation, Inc.

III

Dedication

We dedicate this monograph to our life partners Vasantha Balachandran and Bhama Thiagarajan for their unfailing patience with our long hours and travels and positive encouragement for completion of our work at the sacrifice of family time.

CONTENTS

FOREWORD

For a management tool to be successfully deployed, an objective understanding of its strengths and weaknesses is required. This is especially true for reengineering. From what I have personally experienced, managers often do not fully understand reengineering or its impact on an organization. No wonder people get confused when management's efforts to create change in organizations are constantly referred to as reengineering.

Reengineering today is in a real state of confusion, with many different opinions of its real value. At one extreme, managers view reengineering as a management fad that never got off the ground. Another view is that reengineering provides a convenient explanation for short-term cost-cutting efforts. At the other extreme, managers point to reengineering as the key force behind the strong performance of U.S. industry during the past seven or eight years. As always, the truth lies somewhere in between. But where?

In *Reengineering Revisited,* Bala Balachandran and Ramu Thiagarajan provide a well-articulated analysis of what reengineering is and what it is not. The background section presents a good historical perspective and discusses the promises and challenges of reengineering.

To really understand the impact of reengineering, it is critical to examine concrete examples of reengineering initiatives. The case studies of American Express, IBM, Universal Financial Corporation, Midwest Utility, Pfizer, and my own company, Baxter, offer a range of different approaches and perspectives. Clearly, there is no one correct methodology. However, as presented in the section on "Lessons Learned from BPR Practices," several ingredients are absolutely vital for success.

In my experience, successful reengineering comes down to strong leadership, which has five major components:

- *Setting a clear direction and strategy.* Develop a well-articulated strategy and specific goals that result in a very clear direction for the organization as it embarks on reengineering.

- *Communicate! Communicate! Communicate!* The leader must ensure that everyone on the team understands the importance of the initiative, their specific role, and the support the team can expect from the leader.

- *Motivation, clear prioritization, and incentives.* The leader must make certain the team understands why the reengineering initiative is more important to the company than the hundreds of other "very important priorities" that are competing for resources. Clearly, incentives must be aligned to motivate the team in the desired direction. If the team is charged with "thinking out of the box," taking risks, and shaking up the organization, the leader must make sure specific incentives directly reward that behavior. Without these incentives, the desired changes will not occur.

- *Execution and implementation...making it happen!* The reengineering initiative cannot be viewed simply as a planning exercise. A well-organized plan is important, but the team must understand that execution and implementation are critical.

- *Measurement, assessment, and reassessment.* Finally, the leader must measure the progress made by the team and decide whether changes to the initiative are required. If so, the leader goes back to the first step, and the process continues.

It is clear that successful reengineering is a continuous process. Bala and Ramu state this clearly in the last chapter of the book: "Companies can take a more proactive approach and view change as a continuous process. Such companies will constantly modify their operations to better meet the dynamic needs of the marketplace. For today's companies, change is no longer a one-time reengineering project but an everyday fact of life."

I believe you will enjoy "revisiting" reengineering and the impact it can have on your organization.

Harry Kraemer
President and CEO
Baxter International, Inc.

Business Process Reengineering—
Its History, Promises, and Problems

usiness process reengineering (BPR) has dominated the thinking of corporate executives for much of the 1990s. In 1993, Michael Hammer and James Champy published *Reengineering the Corporation.* According to Hammer and Champy, reengineering was "the fundamental rethinking and radical redesign of business processes to achieve dramatic improvements in critical contemporary measures of performance, such as cost, quality, service, and speed."

A 1994 survey by CSC Index (State of Reengineering Report 1994) found that 69 percent of U.S. companies had some reengineering initiative in place. By 1996, a survey conducted by Louis Harris & Associates revealed that 60 percent of the companies surveyed had undertaken a formal reengineering project in the past two years and that cutting costs was the main reason.

However, we believe that BPR is unlikely to be remembered in the new millennium as the panacea for corporate ills. When Bain & Company, a consulting group, asked executives at 1,000 companies to rate different management tools in 1996, BPR did not score very high. Even the gurus who formalized the idea of BPR acknowledged the difficulty of its implementation.

Historical Perspective

To understand the popularity of BPR initiatives, which peaked in 1993 to 1995, we must understand the economic circumstances under which they were introduced. As a result of value-engineering and cost-cutting initiatives, corporate America had steadily reduced its blue-collar workforce. One reason for this reduction was the replacement of labor with capital; another was the export of labor-intensive operations overseas to countries with cheaper labor. However, the reduction of blue-collar labor did not translate into higher net income; instead, it was largely replaced by white-collar labor in the form of team leaders, technology professionals, consultants, administrators, and others. In fact, the proportion of white-collar labor had been steadily increasing in both the private and public sectors and stood at 54 percent of the total workforce in 1993, according to Strassmann (1995). If the larger white-collar workforce does not increase productivity as much as it adds to costs, then the value added declines. Economic value added (EVA®), defined as net operating profit after taxes minus a capital charge, is a popular measure of a company's earnings. Strassmann's analysis of EVA for the *Fortune* 1,000 U.S. industrial corporations revealed that EVA had been steadily declining over the years. Figure 1 portrays their cumulative EVA from 1984 to 1994.

As is clear from figure 1, the cumulative EVA for the *Fortune* 1,000 was a negative $60 billion in 1985. After three years of increases, there was a steady decline between 1988 and 1991. In 1990, Michael Hammer

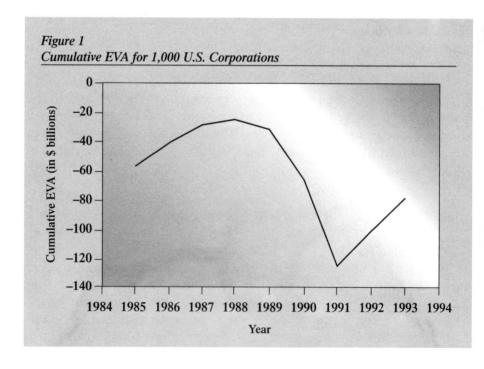

Figure 1
Cumulative EVA for 1,000 U.S. Corporations

published his article "Reengineering Work: Don't Automate, Obliterate." An important reason for this decline was the replacement of the direct costs of labor with the indirect costs of white-collar employment and technology. Even though it appears that EVA increased in later years, Strassman (1995) claims that this is largely attributable to a decrease in the cost of capital, not to an increase in operating income. The decline in productivity and growth and the resulting decline in EVA led corporate America to seek a new management philosophy. In this environment, the radical message of taking an ax and machine gun to the existing organization captured the imagination of the corporate world.

To understand the popularity of BPR, it is important to juxtapose it with other management philosophies. Value engineering was popular in the sixties and seventies, but it did not capture top management's attention. This was partly because, philosophically, value engineering kept the design constant while trying to improve on efficiency and cut costs.

Then came the Japanese waves of "continuous improvement" and "Kaizen costing." The constraint here was the market. Firms adopted the view that market forces dictate prices and tried to optimize costs within that constraint. Hence the term "target costing," meaning that the firm tried to target the costs to be achieved for a given price. Again, this management philosophy did not last, since costs could be cut by only a limited amount.

The next wave was the Total Quality Management (TQM) philosophy of Joseph Juran and W. Edwards Deming. Juran and Deming, both Americans, found little sympathy among Western companies until the success of Japanese companies became apparent. TQM, too, focused on processes, breaking them down into more discrete and simple repetitive tasks, to be performed by less-skilled employees or by more efficient machines. Because of its mechanistic nature and the constraint of keeping the design unchanged, the appeal of TQM was limited.

Thus, due both to the limitations of existing management philosophies and the decline in the value added, BPR's "no-holds-barred" approach was very appealing. The design could be altered and costs could be lowered with no major restrictions. Furthermore, under the rubric of reengineering, companies could undertake massive reductions in labor costs, which were not otherwise possible. In particular, it was possible to eliminate significant layers of middle management that had built up in the eighties and early nineties, contributing to the decline of corporate productivity in the standard metrics of performance, such as EVA and net income. Reengineering was touted as a panacea for corporate evils.

Promises of Reengineering

Analogous to zero-based budgeting, reengineering held promise for large-scale innovation, because of its "clean-sheet" approach or "out-of-the-box thinking" about processes and functions. This idea of radical rethinking, indeed, was the reason for the dramatic improvements in several processes, such as the accounts payable function in Ford, product development in Kodak, and credit processing in IBM. The underlying premise behind reengineering is also laudable because the goal is to "have an organization flexible enough to beat any competitor's price, innovative enough to keep its products and services technologically fresh and dedicated enough to deliver maximum quality and customer service" (Hammer and Champy 1993, p. 7). But these goals have some internal inconsistencies. For example, it is hard to beat the competitor's price if you want to have maximum quality and customer service and loyalty, since these attributes come at a price that the company will have to pass on to the consumer.

The second advantage of reengineering was the notion that the efficiency of the whole organization depends on the efficiency of the parts. Thus, employees were made aware that unless each process was tightened, it would be very difficult, if not impossible, to have an efficiently performing organization. BPR fostered awareness of how each process fits into the organization as a whole. Employees were encouraged to understand what they were doing so that they could ask, "Why are we doing it?"

Third, employees and management were made aware of the major forces for the success of the organization: customers, competition, and change. However, we would like to add a fourth "C": costs. In other words, success on the first three dimensions comes at a cost.

The BPR initiative had technological underpinnings. It encouraged the replacement of labor with technology and the provision of more and better information to make processes more efficient. Inventions and technological innovations such as bar-coding, optical scanning, and electronic data interchange also permitted radical redesign. As an additional benefit to the firm, employees were encouraged to think in terms of technology substituting for labor.

Besides introducing the concept that the success of the organization depended on its parts, reengineering fostered the thinking that tasks are multidimensional and that it is dysfunctional to think in terms of silos. Companies lose focus when managers think about only their departments or employees think simply in terms of their jobs. In fact, part of the reason for the growth in the white-collar jobs was firms strengthening these silos, leading to power struggles between departments. The IBM case study reveals that because of silos, eight different sales groups approached the customer with different incentives and packages, resulting in a confused customer and, eventually, lost business.

Finally, BPR emphasized the main success factors: core customers, processes, competencies, distribution systems, and costs.

Challenges of Reengineering

The challenges of BPR were many. First, the approach was very radical, as Michael Hammer's rhetoric demonstrates:

- "In this journey, we'll carry our wounded and shoot the dissenters...." *Forbes,* September 13, 1993.

- "Reengineering must be initiated...by someone who has...enough status to break legs...." *Planning Review,* May/June 1993.

- "Don't try to forestall reengineering. If senior management is serious about reengineering they'll shoot you." *Management Review,* September 1993.

While this had its advantages in bringing "shock value" to what might otherwise have been a complacent organization, it resulted in a rapid loss of what had been built over many years: human capital and employee loyalty. This is because some corporate executives used BPR as an excuse for indiscriminate downsizing.

Downsizing may have positive effects for the short term, but without revenue growth, it is unlikely to have positive effects in the longer term. In fact, a study by Dwight Gertz of Mercer Management of 800 major U.S. companies found that 145 of them used cost-cutting to reach profit levels above their industry benchmarks, but only 23 percent of these firms were able to make the switch to revenue growth (*Wall Street Journal*, 1996).

Employee morale is necessary for long-term sustained sales growth, but BPR, used as a cost-cutting tool, had a severely negative effect on employee morale without having any compensatory long-term benefit. Pankaj Ghemawat, a Harvard Business School professor, observed, "Wall Street won't pay anymore for raising profit margins on a stagnant sales base. The crucial issue has become how far does the company stretch for growth" (*Wall Street Journal*, 1996).

Because of the lack of focus on revenue growth, indiscriminate cost-cutting with middle management as the target resulted in "corporate anorexia," comparable to radical approaches to losing weight. In a systematic approach to weight loss through dieting and exercise, the loss of weight is likely to be small, steady, and gradual. In a radical approach, there can be a large weight loss with dangerous or crippling consequences. Drastic cost-cutting without enhanced revenue growth had similar effects.

Second, because BPR was defined in generic terms, companies started calling all their management initiatives "reengineering," partly because they lacked a proper explanation of what reengineering is. Thus, both successes and failures (of which there were many) were blamed on reengineering.

Perhaps the single biggest shortcoming of BPR is its focus within the organization—what we call "intracompany" BPR. A corporation does not exist in a vacuum. It needs to be concerned about its markets, its shareholders, and its customers, as well as its employees and processes. But BPR ignored cultural aspects and other issues that go into the development and growth of a corporation. This was also the reason for the lack of focus on growing revenue in many BPR initiatives.

However, we believe that reengineering should focus on what we call "intercompany" BPR. Reengineering as a philosophy is sound, but when companies keep its focus internal, it is likely to fail. It is important to understand the roles of markets, employee morale, customers, and especially corporate culture and commitment in initiating and developing BPR. We have focused our analysis of the case-study companies toward this end and designed our questionnaire and interviews to gain insights on these important dimensions.

2

Lessons from Survey Analysis

As indicated in chapter 1, one of the goals of this project was to undertake an analysis of both intracompany and intercompany BPR. We wanted to understand the issues within the company in terms of cost control and the issues relating to customers, suppliers, and others. To ensure the broadest possible sample for our survey, we undertook a widespread search of possible BPR candidates. We searched the following databases for possible candidates:

- All sources listed in the Dow Jones News Survey;
- All sources listed in Lexis-Nexis News;
- All disclosures in the financial statements over 1984 through 1996 from the Dialog database; and
- Participants in the J.L. Kellogg Graduate School of Management's program on business process reengineering.

An exhaustive search of these sources yielded 680 firms that have undertaken reengineering initiatives. We sent a letter with a sample survey (appendix A) to each of these firms. About 150 firms responded. Some of these firms claimed that they had used the term "reengineering" somewhat loosely and that there was no serious BPR initiative in place. After eliminating all the invalid responses, we obtained 83 valid responses from several different industries, such as financial services, drug manufacturing, telecommunications, electric utilities, and computer manufacturing. Furthermore, the reengineering initiatives ranged from simple processes such as payroll to firm-wide reengineering. We present below the results of the responses classified into three major areas:

- Before reengineering
- During and after reengineering
- Evaluation of the reengineering initiatives

Before Reengineering

Why reengineer?

Reengineering, in its broadest sense, is a comprehensive overhaul of a company's processes, culture, strategy, and organization. More than 90 percent of the executives surveyed believe that the primary motives for reengineering projects at their organizations were the underlying inefficiencies in processes and the lack of viability of their existing cost structures. The next most important motive appears to be declining margins. Clearly these motives are related, and it appears that inefficient operations resulting in higher costs and hence declining margins are the major trigger for BPR. Figure 2 highlights the major reasons executives in our survey cited for reengineering.

The response that high cost and inefficient processes trigger BPR initiatives is telling. A big part of this management philosophy involves controlling costs and making processes efficient. As indicated in chapter 1, BPR appeared at a time of declining value added. With eroding profit margins, an easy area for management to target is what we call "middle-line minimization." Reducing costs without sacrificing revenue was the lofty goal of BPR.

How long did the situation last that created the need for BPR?

BPR projects typically start only after executives determine that the underlying problem is not short-term; in nearly two-thirds of the cases, the underlying issue had been observed for more than two years. Only in a very small percentage of the cases did management wait longer before beginning a BPR initiative.

What other alternatives were considered?

Our survey revealed that outsourcing, restructuring, and overhauling employee incentive schemes were frequently considered potential alternatives to BPR (figure 3). It should be noted, however, that these

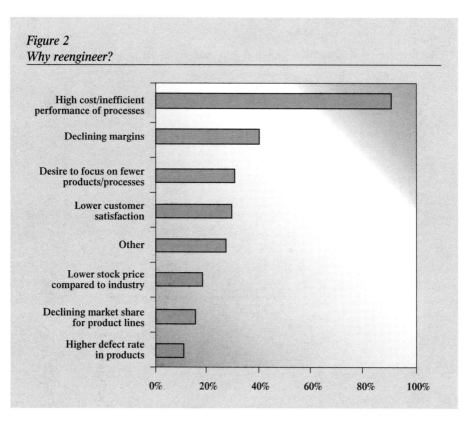

Figure 2
Why reengineer?

alternatives were exclusive of the BPR initiative. Put differently, outsourcing was frequently an outcome of the BPR initiative. It is interesting to note, however, that the popular concept of EVA was considered as an alternative in only 20 percent of the cases, partly because EVA is a measurement system and is not directly related to the efficiency of the processes.

Why were other alternatives rejected?

Figure 4 reveals, however, that these alternatives to BPR were rejected mainly because they were either too expensive or too difficult to implement. This gives rise to the need for costly external consultants.

Figure 3
What other alternatives were considered instead of BPR?

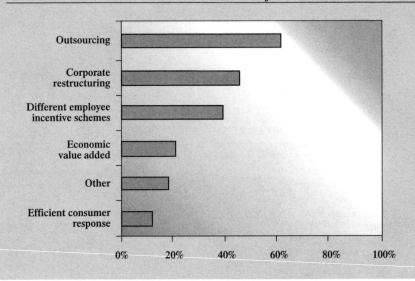

Figure 4
Why were other alternatives rejected?

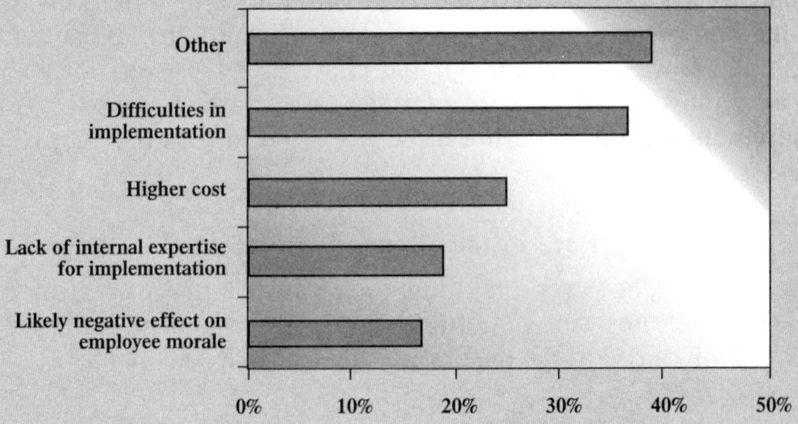

During and after Reengineering

What functional areas/processes were reengineered?

As figure 5 shows, a large proportion of reengineering projects tended to focus on the purchasing and inventory control portions of the supply chain. Customer service was another area that underwent a significant overhaul. Thus, the focus was either a supply push (inventory management) or a demand pull. An absence of inventory control and lack of good processes for purchases is frequently cited as an important reason for rising costs and declining margins. Another area that contributed to higher costs is declining customer service.

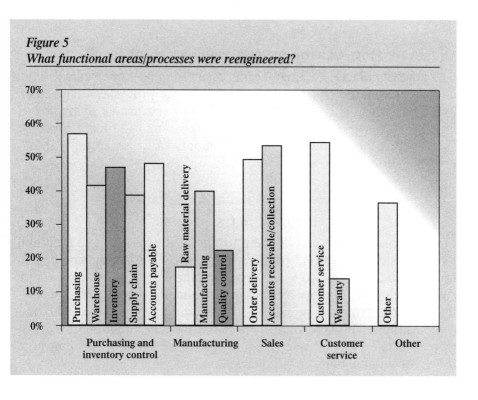

Figure 5
What functional areas/processes were reengineered?

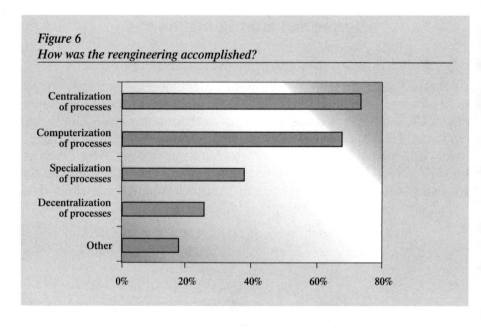

Figure 6
How was the reengineering accomplished?

How was the reengineering accomplished?

In a majority of cases, reengineering resulted in both the centralization and the automation or computerization of the processes being examined (figure 6). This is not surprising, since the use of technology is integral to reengineering. Furthermore, reducing redundant processes is frequently the impetus behind BPR initiatives. This naturally leads to centralization of processes.

Why were outside consultants employed in the program?

Outside consultants were valued for their BPR expertise and their ability to provide an external perspective (figure 7). Also, outside consultants can be expected to know the best practices and thus provide the right benchmark. A large number of respondents—nearly 50 percent—hired consultants to validate efforts already in place in their organizations. This is not surprising, since the CEO might perceive outside expertise as more objective and thus more valuable. Furthermore, using consultants helps avoid internal politics.

What, if any, degree of disruption occurred in the workplace during the implementation of the BPR program?

Workforce disruption was fairly extensive during BPR implementation. About 50 percent of the respondents indicated a reasonable amount of disruption because of the BPR efforts. Given that BPR initiatives are major and involve several processes, this response is not surprising. Of our 83 responses, only 5 had fewer than four processes under reengineering initiatives.

How much, if any, organizational restructuring occurred as a result of the BPR program?

One reason for the disruption is the extent of the restructuring. More than 50 percent of our sample firms indicated that significant restructuring accompanied the BPR effort. The axiom behind BPR efforts is "radical redesign," which is not possible without significant restructuring. Figure 8 shows the results of our survey responses that ranked the

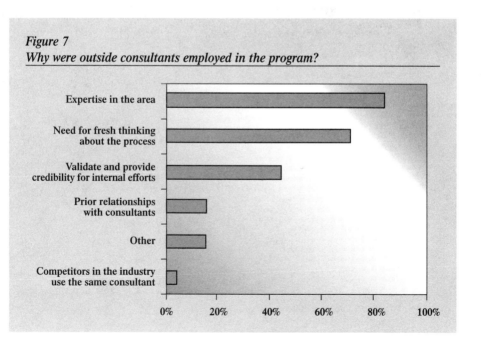

Figure 7
Why were outside consultants employed in the program?

restructuring on a five-point scale, with five indicating a major restructuring. More than 50 percent of the respondents indicated a rank of 3 or above.

Evaluation of the Reengineering Initiatives

What was the effect on employee morale during the implementation of the BPR program?

Among other things, people are generally influenced by two major psychological factors—fear and greed. In the initial stages of BPR, fear tends to dominate, whereas in the later stages, greed tends to dominate. While the morale of the average sample firm is neither predominantly

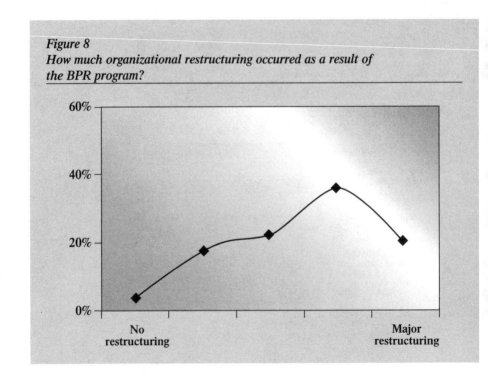

Figure 8
How much organizational restructuring occurred as a result of the BPR program?

positive nor negative, comments from the survey indicate that correlation with the perceived (or actual) success reveals that the morale was much higher for firms with a higher perceived success rate.

What assurances did management provide regarding the employees' job situation?

In about two-thirds of the cases, management provided no assurances to employees about their job situation following reengineering. This partly reflects the fact that U.S. corporations believe in hiring and firing as needed. Since BPR is partly an effort to cut costs, it is not surprising that few assurances were provided. Figure 9 indicates that severance pay or relocation to other units within the organization was used as a carrot in a little over a third of the companies.

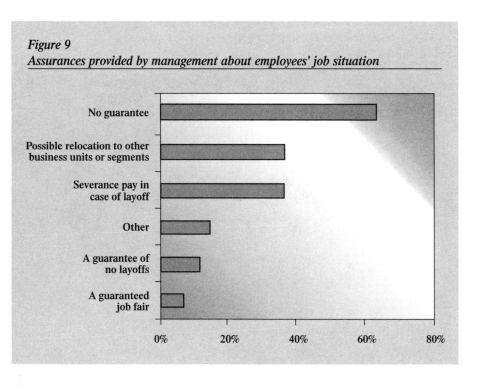

Figure 9
Assurances provided by management about employees' job situation

What changes in the compensation structure and performance evaluation took place as a result of the BPR program?

Figure 10 indicates that only 27 percent of all the sample firms did not change their compensation structures. In interviews with the companies, we found that senior management realized that it is difficult to motivate employees without some incentives in terms of changes in the compensation structure. As indicated earlier, some BPR initiatives were accompanied by EVA initiatives with the compensation of the management tied closely to measurement of value-added or cost savings. Radical redesign, which is integral to BPR initiatives, requires significant adjustment on the part of employees, and this is very costly. It is difficult to require employees to change their ways of thinking without offering significant incentives.

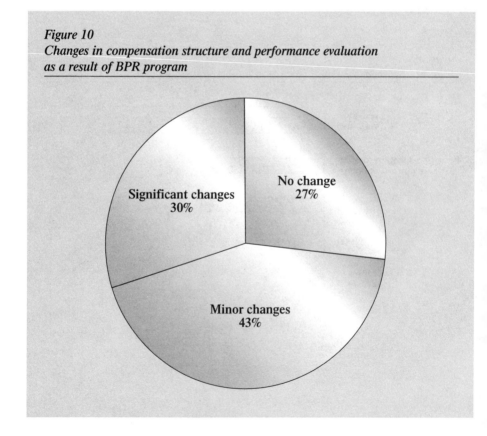

Figure 10
Changes in compensation structure and performance evaluation
as a result of BPR program

Were the goals of the BPR program accomplished?

Perhaps the most important question for management is whether this initiative met its goals. Only about half of the respondents (57 percent) indicated that the benefits had exceeded the cost of BPR initiatives. The next-largest response was "difficult to evaluate" (29 percent). Part of this was due to the fact that the improvements, if any, are nonfinancial. Such results are inherently not quantifiable, but more than half of the respondents thought BPR was beneficial. A small percentage indicated that cost exceeded benefits. In most of these cases, the problem was absence of commitment or integration with other departments, or the problem of consultants assuming ownership of the project. This finding was confirmed in our interviews. Figure 11 provides the breakdown of the responses.

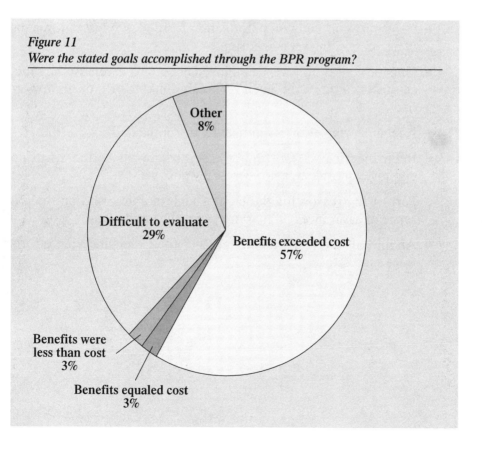

Figure 11
Were the stated goals accomplished through the BPR program?

Summary

The survey analysis reveals the following major points:

- Reengineering was initiated because of the high cost of processes and low customer satisfaction.

- This problem lasted for about two years before reengineering initiatives began.

- Other alternatives, such as EVA and restructuring, were considered but rejected because of lack of internal expertise, higher cost, or difficulty in implementation.

- Purchasing and inventory control were the processes most often reengineered. The other major area was customer service.

- Centralization and computerization were very important means of accomplishing reengineering.

- Outside consultants were employed about 50 percent of the time, chiefly because of the need for fresh thinking or industry expertise.

- Reengineering efforts significantly disrupted daily operations.

- Reengineering was not totally embraced by all, so the effect on employee morale was not especially positive.

- Part of the reason for the lack of high morale could be the absence of assurances or guarantees for the employees.

- About half the respondents felt that their reengineering efforts were successful.

Case Studies

American Express Company

Company Name: American Express Company	Ticker: NYSE: AXP
Project Name: The Challenge for Change	

Functional Areas Covered: • Finance (Global Operations) Savings: • $269 million by the end of 1996	Financial Performance Represents reengineering applied to global finance. Additional reengineering in other areas continues at American Express.

Key Strengths: • Standardization • Executive sponsorship • Incentive/reward structure • Communication • Patience/long-term perspective	Obstacles: • Divisional/geographic boundaries • Market shifts • Low tolerance for risk • Resistance to change

Comment:
"American Express transformed itself into a far more likeable enterprise—the customers like them, the merchants like them, their employees like them, and their shareholders surely like them."

History and Background

American Express is no stranger to tough markets and change. Formed in 1850 when Henry Wells merged Wells & Company with other express carriers, namely Livingston & Fargo and Butterfield, Wasson & Company, the American Express Company began a long tradition of adapting to better face the market. The modern company, while operating globally in the information age, is no exception. In order to compete in current markets, American Express is focused on three key levers for growth:

- *Opening its card network* – American Express is challenging the duopoly of Visa and MasterCard by opening its card network to banks and other institutions.

- *Expanding financial service businesses* – The company's goal is to become as widely known for financial services as it is for providing card and travel services. The company provides financial services and products, including financial planning, small business services, brokerage services, mutual funds, and insurance.

- *Expand internationally* – The third piece of the company's strategy is to bring its financial and travel expertise, services, and products to more markets around the globe.

These lofty goals required a rethinking of its business. Over its history, American Express has not been bound to the same strategy, but has been innovative in the face of stiff competition. In the past, the company has shed operating units, rapidly formed new business units, and acquired non-overlapping businesses in attempts to reinvent itself. Reengineering represented another chapter in a long story about a company that was continuously transforming.

Origins of the Problem/Recognition of the Opportunity

In 1991, the company recognized that there was a problem. The United States was facing a recession that dramatically changed many markets. Companies began pruning their workforces, especially the white-collar, middle manager ranks, as markets shrank and competition intensified.

Like many others, American Express, the blue-chip financial and travel services company, was severely affected. In this dynamic time, some of what differentiated the organization from its competition had been lost. Customers began to view American Express-like offerings as commodities.

Through a slow evolutionary process, the company had become too transaction-bound and was unable to respond quickly to changes in its markets. As earnings went into a tailspin (see company profile), stockholders joined customers in their demand for higher quality at lower costs. American Express heard the wakeup call. Leadership recognized that the ground rules had to change. Operating protocols would have to be reinvented. While all facets of the company embraced the need to reengineer their core processes, the finance function addressed this drive to recreate the business with an initiative known internally as the "The Challenge for Change"—a plan to transform the global finance group. Their mission went beyond competing in present markets. They wanted to be in a position to help define future ones. By being proactive instead of reactive, American Express Finance took up the mantra "Reengineering Ahead of the Curve." Given the company's situation, nothing less than a radical transformation of the finance business was warranted.

Implementation Issues

Within any organization, reengineering initiatives consistently set lofty goals (delight customers, increase profitability, reduce time to market, etc.). Establishing targets is fundamental to reengineering, although actually reaching them can take many forms. American Express took a holistic approach, not relying on a single set of focused improvements but, instead, touching on a number of aspects of the business as it engaged in the "The Challenge for Change."

Organization

American Express had become dominated by a regional organizational structure. In addition, its workforce identified tightly with certain products. It was the classic case of workers adopting very narrow views and operating within silos. Business units and geographic regions did not work well together. Because of the failures and problems of working across uncoordinated lines, certain individuals had been established as rework specialists, who focused on dealing with these problems. American Express had a formal, traditional hierarchy, with all the issues of communication and responsiveness that bureaucracies perpetuate. The structure bred inefficiency, redundancy, and an inward focus. It took a lot for the company to first recognize that a problem existed, but responding to the new challenge was even more difficult. For the American Express organization, there was quite a chasm to cross.

The project easily identified opportunities to eliminate duplication in processes that resulted from product line, functional, or geographic focus. One of the early goals was to mirror customers' needs more closely. The result of the organizational and functional redesign was to reduce 46 different operating venues to only 3 Centers of Excellence, where the processes are nearly always consistent. For example, it is now possible to transfer an employee from the Phoenix, Arizona, Financial Resource Center (FRC) to another FRC in New Delhi, India, and to have that person productive almost immediately, since the processes in both sites are identical. Obviously, supporting far fewer operations creates economies of scale, reducing costs and improving the bottom line. More focused operations also increased flexibility and allowed for consistent quality and seamless customer service for American Express.

Culture

The product line, functional, and geographic focus created enormous conflicts of interest within the organization. It was difficult to focus on the needs of customers or challenges of competitors when concerns were focused internally. Bent on defense, employees' thinking had become stifled, and the discussion focused on what comprised the "as is" state. The collective energy was wasted on legacy processes and systems. Customer service, profitability, and employee morale suffered.

Financial transaction processing at American Express is run as a business and led by general managers and their supporting teams. The company relies heavily on teamwork to get the day-to-day work done. American Express has also emphasized and improved reward and recognition systems to motivate positive behavior. The result has been a more highly productive, integrated organization. No longer internally focused, the collective attention has been turned to meeting the needs of customers, shareholders, and, importantly, the employees themselves. Problems happen less frequently and are solved faster. Service levels and financial management controls have also dramatically improved.

Technology

American Express, like many companies, has achieved cost and time savings, as well as data accessibility and integrity, from the consolidation of home-grown legacy systems. For American Express, this consolidation represented an opportunity to utilize good data management to provide meaningful information more quickly. The power of linking data previously housed in separate systems had been underestimated.

Processes

American Express was performing major processes redundantly across the company. Activities like general accounting, expense analysis, advertising control, and report preparation, to name a few, were completed in an uncoordinated fashion. The consolidation of these duplicated processes represented a real opportunity. Consolidation resulted in increased flexibility, standardization, reduction in overhead, fewer control points, and streamlined systems and organizations. In the end, all of the process improvements, even deep within the back office, resulted in better customer service for American Express.

Applying a process mindset negated some of the ills that silo thinking imposed on the company over the years. It forced many organizations within the company to look at their work through the eyes of the customer.

Evaluation and Follow-up

"The Challenge for Change" was unanimously heralded as a success inside and out of American Express. By every measure, the result of the reengineering efforts is a global finance organization that provides a higher service delivery level at much lower cost. The impact can be felt in the bottom line, with savings that amounted to more than $260 million as of year-end 1996 (figure 12).

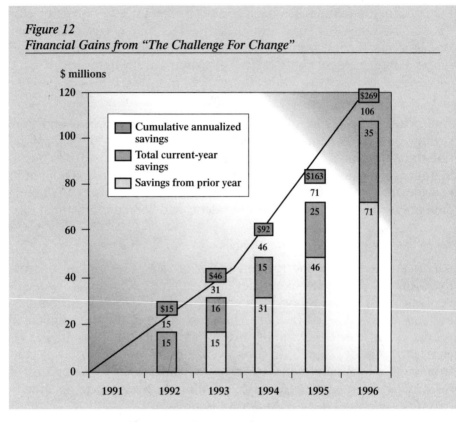

Figure 12
Financial Gains from "The Challenge For Change"

For American Express, the initiative was more than introducing novel processes or applying slick new tools to the business. The company underwent a fundamental shift in the way it viewed the business. Finance moved itself out of the obscurity of the back office and became a proactive, quality- and value-added contributor to the business. Performance within the finance organization was connected to improving customer service and increasing profitability for the company's shareholders.

While the positive effect of reengineering is evident in the new organization structure, its effect on employees should be highlighted, too. Employees stress that they enjoy their work more. Before reengineering, many employees viewed themselves within strict functional, divisional, and geographic silos.

At the individual level, "The Challenge for Change" has expanded the opportunities for finance personnel. They now use terminology like risk-taker and challenger to describe themselves. Their jobs now demand greater creativity and problem solving. Many commented that they enjoy greater control over their workday and feel they are making larger contributions to the company. No longer thinking in terms of silos, each person now focuses on the customer and claims enterprise loyalty. "The Challenge for Change" enabled personal and professional growth across the organization. It is important to note that American Express employees are happier people since reengineering.

Reengineering was a difficult path to travel for global finance, but American Express found the destination well worthwhile. What it learned from its reengineering experience is now being shared across other parts of the company. The potential benefit is staggering.

Key Lessons

The difficult competitive position of 1991 turned out to be a blessing. Without the crisis, it would have been nearly impossible to generate the motivation required. Given the company's circumstances, everyone understood the need to reengineer the business. The success of most reengineering efforts depends on a clear, compelling motivation that every part of the organization can understand. At American Express, employees, executives, and stakeholders alike agreed that the system was broken.

American Express did not consider expensive information systems or complicated best practice processes key to its success. The company stressed the following fundamental elements as critical to the success of its reengineering endeavors:

- *Executive sponsorship.* By placing responsibility for the success of its reengineering activities at the very highest levels, American Express was able to implement more dramatic change in less time. Naming top executives as champions for "The Challenge for Change" signaled to the entire organization how committed the company needed to be to transform the business. This top-level support enabled obstacles to be quickly overcome, garnered needed but scarce resources, and kept the project focused on moving in the right direction.

- *Consistent, continuous communication.* Members of the business transformation team repeatedly emphasized the importance of communication. Change is difficult, but it is nearly impossible if employees do not comprehend why it is necessary and where it will lead them. It is also important to create a common language through which communication can take place. For example, participants need to see the positive effects of change through understandable targets and related performance metrics. Too often in large corporations, communication is assumed and appears simple. In fact, often the connection between sender and receiver across these large organizations is never made. Either the message is never sent or the recipient misunderstands it. In any case, communication fails and the desired change never occurs.

- *A keen understanding of the humanistic effects on the organization and the culture.* After reengineering was initiated, the roles people played and the ways they related to one other were altered. American Express recognized that realigning the organization still required that all constituencies remain in alignment as they moved toward "The Challenge for Change" goals. Management knew that the organization would suffer emotional ups and downs as it struggled with the project. Leaders of the initiative focused on eliminating uncertainty, because they believed "uncertainty bred dysfunctional behavior and pessimism would reign until certainty was in sight." American Express also found that the organization valued having a symbol for its new identity.

- *Breaking down geographic/business unit silos.* In a simple physical way, this meant removing the walls between departments and divisions in every office. American Express adopted an open floor plan with no offices at its Financial Resource Centers. Besides removing private offices, "The Challenge for Change" resulted in a significant shake-up in the organizational structure of finance at American Express. It was an opportunity for the company to leverage the scale of operations worldwide. Employees had identified themselves with a geographic or business unit first, and this led to large variations and process inefficiency. By consolidating operations, moving to standard processes, and bringing the employees together around a single mission, American Express recognized substantial benefits. The office in New Delhi is the same as the office in Phoenix, Arizona, or Burgess Hill, England— same office layout, same processes, and employees working to the same end.

- *Links to incentive and reward structure.* Adopting "The Challenge for Change" also meant making performance-based incentives a much larger portion of overall compensation. The proper reward structure solidified aligning the interests of the employee with those of American Express. Obviously, this provided the project needed attention and commitment throughout the organization. It also enabled the initiative to spur the best and brightest of the company to dedicate themselves full-time to the project. By "putting their money where their mouths were," American Express clearly established its commitment to reengineering success.

- *Patience and time.* While the results are dramatic, they only come through hard work and focused discipline. American Express is a large company and has a long corporate tradition. An important ingredient in changing all of that is time. Retaining the collective will to change and conviction about reengineering was a real "Challenge to Change" (figure 13).

The journey American Express took with reengineering was not an easy one. It required commitment, communication, and significant resources over a long period to be successful. The path seems difficult, but the destination is worth the trip.

Figure 13
American Express Now and in the Future

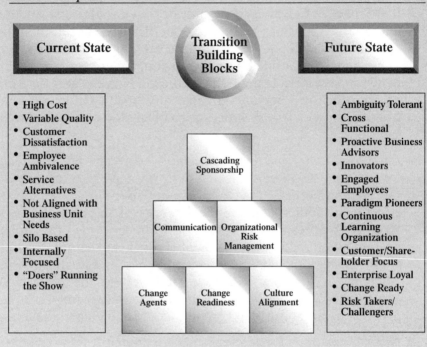

Current State	Transition Building Blocks	Future State
• High Cost • Variable Quality • Customer Dissatisfaction • Employee Ambivalence • Service Alternatives • Not Aligned with Business Unit Needs • Silo Based • Internally Focused • "Doers" Running the Show	Cascading Sponsorship Communication · Organizational Risk Management Change Agents · Change Readiness · Culture Alignment	• Ambiguity Tolerant • Cross Functional • Proactive Business Advisors • Innovators • Engaged Employees • Paradigm Pioneers • Continuous Learning Organization • Customer/Shareholder Focus • Enterprise Loyal • Change Ready • Risk Takers/Challengers

IBM Corporation

Company Name: **IBM Corporation**	Ticker: **NYSE: IBM**

Project Name:
Business Transformation

Functional Areas Covered:
- Finance
- Operations (Supply Chain, Fulfillment)
- Sales
- Purchasing
- Research & Development
- Information Technology
- Services

Savings:
- Rebounded from an $8.1 billion loss
- Reduced days sales outstanding
- Order to delivery cycle times compressed
- Higher inventory turns

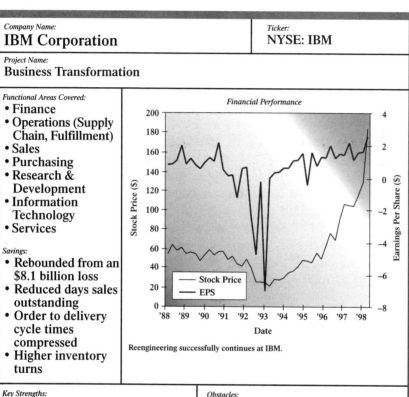

Financial Performance

Reengineering successfully continues at IBM.

Key Strengths:
- Simplification and globalization of processes
- Senior management leadership
- Rewards based on results
- Integration of business units
- Customer-focused view

Obstacles:
- Divisional/geographic boundaries
- Market shifts
- Low tolerance for risk
- Resistance to change

Comment:
"It had to be done. The world around us, the computer industry IBM had dominated with its mainframe presence, had changed and we had to catch up."

History and Background

As the new millennium approaches, it is hard to believe that one of the dominant players in modern technology actually got its start at the turn of the last century. In 1890, the Census Bureau held a contest to find a more accurate way of counting the waves of new immigrants and accurately measuring the growing population. The winner was Herman Hollerith, a Census Bureau statistician, who had invented a punch card tabulating machine that could accurately keep a running total. From this invention grew a business that eventually merged with two other tabulating enterprises to form the Computing-Tabulating-Recording (C-T-R) Company in 1911. It was not until Thomas Watson took the reins of C-T-R in 1914, after being the number two executive at National Cash Register, that the company began its ascent. As the company grew and began establishing a worldwide presence, the name was changed to International Business Machines (IBM). Watson's enthusiasm and professional practices created loyal employees and loyal customers, giving rise to the belief "Nobody ever got fired for buying an IBM." IBM's success has been attributed to Watson's emphasis on the customer.

Throughout this century, IBM has led the charge of computing with such innovations as System/360, the IBM PC, the ThinkPad laptop, and its support of network computing. But even IBM, whose commitment to research produced four Nobel Prize winners, had difficulty keeping pace with the tidal wave of technological change that characterizes the high-tech arena. The eighties and early nineties proved a difficult time for Big Blue. The company admits to being rocked by two back-to-back revolutions—the proliferation of the PC and the move toward client/server computing. Both changed how and where computers were used. The rules under which IBM had led the industry no longer applied. The IBM tradition was called into question when the company reported a loss of $8 billion in 1993.

By all accounts, IBM is undergoing a revolution. It is a company of 270,000 employees reshaping the way they work and respond to their dynamic environment. With drastic cost cutting, layoffs, and a new leader, Louis Gerstner, from outside the old hierarchy, IBM survived and once again emerged a leader. Even after these challenges, IBM remains the world's largest supplier of hardware and software.

Origins of the Problem/Recognition of the Opportunity

IBM's wake-up call came in the form of a devastating $8.1 billion loss in 1993. One executive stated, "We had become a company with 250,000 employees and no bottom line." IBM, the beacon of the American high-tech industry, found itself overwhelmed in a market it no longer recognized, as the move away from mainframes toward PCs and client/server computing spelled a drastic change in direction for the industry. The big question both inside and outside the company was whether the monolithic corporation should be broken into smaller, independent organizations.

Probably the strongest indicator of the illness IBM experienced was the change in its traditionally loyal customer base. As the buying decision for many computer products moved from the centralized purchasing department to the decentralized end-user departments, IBM's strong sales force discovered it had no way to reach this multitude of new consumers.

In recounting the dark days, IBM employees describe an organization that had lost vision. The company had to take drastic action and eliminated its practice of full employment, laying off people for the first time. Employees were being let go as share price and earnings fell; customers were leaving as cheaper, more innovative competitors appeared on the scene daily.

For a variety of reasons, both competitive and cultural, IBM had built up massive redundancies. In fact, there were once 500,000 different profit measures for the company. IBM had 250,000 employees at that time, giving each employee two measures of profit! Some compared IBM's experience to a heart attack after years of a fatty diet and no exercise.

3

Implementation Issues

IBM engaged in an evolutionary reengineering process. Early on (1994–1995), the name of the game was cost reduction. Taking an external focus, IBM benchmarked itself against the competition and other industries to figure out where excesses might lie. This benchmarking led to the redesign of some of its core processes to reduce expenses. Initially, much energy was spent identifying where some leverage might be gained by sharing resources and moving toward commonality. One manager said, "It wasn't about different or better, it was about having just one [process]."

The second phase (1996–1997) involved deployment. What had been learned about combining processes and eliminating obvious non-value-added activities was now applied throughout the greater organization. There was a big move to make sure certain processes were performed in a common way across the enterprise.

The current phase (1998 on) involves the integration of processes and information systems leading to e-business. Traditional handoffs and boundaries between functions and operating units are being called into question and rationalized. "We were the best army in the world, but we would kill each other off before we got to battle," remarked a senior executive. IBM's clearly stated strategy is to work cooperatively, while keeping the focus on the customer.

Reengineering at IBM was a monumental undertaking and had a profound impact. The following framework identifies the key activities of IBM's Business Transformation initiative.

Organization

One quarter of a million people work for IBM, along with an immense number of corporate and government entities that count themselves as customers, and the organization is correspondingly complex. Appointing Gerstner as an agent of change at the top has unquestionably transformed IBM to a large degree. IBM reorganized itself to place more emphasis on the customer as well as manage the business better. It views its business along four dimensions: customer view (finance, telecommunications, original equipment manufacturing, etc.), brand view (RS/6000, networking hardware, Lotus, etc.), channel view (IBM direct, value added retailers, retail, etc.), and geographic view (regions, countries, etc.). Each of these dimensions intersects with the others. When a utility company on the West Coast wishes to purchase Lotus Notes through IBM Direct, putting the product into the customer's hands requires cooperation across many parts of IBM. IBM believes this is the best way to manage the business—with the emphasis on customer and brand.

Culture

For a long time, the conservative dark suits and white shirts worn by the IBM workforce were a company trademark. In an environment of start-up companies and rapid innovation, many questioned whether IBM's traditional approach, once considered a benefit, might now spell its doom. During the period when IBM suffered severe losses and cutbacks, many of the corporate tenets were either violated or thrown out. Many employees who had spent nearly all of their working lives with the organization hardly recognized the new IBM. Determined to maintain its position in the industry, IBM implemented a management system that drove continuous improvement, set aggressive and measurable targets, and broke apart fiefdoms by taking cross-functional approaches to its business problems. Throughout the entire organization, every employee had new, aligned objectives. The reward system was synchronized to occur simultaneously for everyone. Some resisted this pervasive change. The line employees adopted new practices quickly, but some managers went kicking and screaming, IBM's culture is now founded on teaming effectively and working collectively.

Technology

Even though IBM is one of the premier providers of technology to businesses throughout the world, the company had room to improve on this front. Through the Business Transformation initiative, the number of data centers was reduced from 155 to 28. The 31 private data networks have been subsumed by a single end-to-end wide area network. The focus on the information technology side was to provide efficient and effective tools that connected every part of the organization. Collaboration was key, and the knowledge management tools created important connections in the sharing of information. Not surprisingly, IBM is the world's largest user of Lotus Notes, with more than 200,000 clients (IBM acquired Lotus Corporation in 1995). Key to IBM's current strategy for growth is leveraging the knowledge and experience that resides within its vast organization. The tools of technology are fundamental to achieving that vision.

Like many other large corporations engaged in reengineering, IBM has some limited implementation of SAP's R/3 to automate transaction processing in some business units. The cost and length of time required to migrate all of IBM's legacy data to a single SAP platform are prohibitive. IBM has found that in some new applications, such as Storage System Division or procurement, the transition to SAP is faster than for established operations.

In general, standardizing IBM's applications became an exercise of choosing the best among the existing systems. Once cost reduction from consolidation was exhausted, the company turned to thinking about better, more effective ways of using its systems infrastructure. IBM began to focus on its ability to take the data collected through its many systems and *analyze* it. Using common applications and a common development workbench or platform, IBM set out to build data warehouses. These warehouses provide a single source of data, operate on common data definitions, improve data accuracy, and allow a more global view of the business. These systems are providing greater access to data on a more timely basis. Standard and custom views, ad hoc queries, the ability to roll or drill down into the data, and the ability to link to other applications have enabled IBM to use its information resources to improve the business.

Processes

When IBM realized that it was losing money, its first move was to cut costs and reduce the amount of time it took to perform various processes. As with its systems initiatives, IBM moved to consolidate processes and take advantage of its scale. The company reduced its product line from 3,000 different PC models to 150, and instead of using eight different power supplies in the various ThinkPads (laptops), the current design is standardized upon one. As the company moved to restructure the organization, it realized significant value by simplifying its processes.

While IBM worked on increasing efficiency and reducing cost, it also had to worry about improving customer satisfaction. Through exceptional skill management software, the company is able to deliver the right skill at the right time to its customers. By using knowledge management and intellectual capital management, it increased its win rate in the consulting business by more than 40 percent. Before reengineering, more than 65 percent of all shipments were behind schedule. IBM also found itself being undercut by much smaller, more responsive competitors. New processes speed product to market at a lower cost. The company is now able to provide the customers with what they want, when they want it, and at a price they are willing to pay. Processes are now structured to make it easier for customers to do business with IBM.

Evaluation and Follow-up

IBM accomplished its goal and indeed transformed its business. The company has forever changed. The appointment of Louis Gerstner, an outsider and strategic thinker, broke with tradition. He brought a different set of expectations to the company and infused its staid culture with a new perspective. When the company set out to reinvent itself, Gerstner showed that he was serious by placing the responsibility for the reengineering initiative under its most senior management. IBM was going to transform the way it conducted business or die trying.

The list of victories is long and comes from many different parts of the organization:

- Reduced delivery cycle
- Improved inventory turns
- Lowered fulfillment transaction costs
- Reduced corporate days sales outstanding
- Reduced hardware development time
- Reduced number of computer models
- Reduced cost of production materials
- Reduced cost of nonproduction materials

- Decreased financial close from 18 to 7 days
- Reduced finance and accounting expense
- Reduced IT costs

There is little doubt that IBM is more efficient as a result of reengineering, but the gains are actually more profound with the level of increased innovation. IBM is bringing new products to market faster, and these new products are of a higher quality and meet the needs of customers better than ever before. IBM is winning where it counts—the customer's purchase. There is balance between being effective—maximizing revenue and making the customer happy—and being efficient—driving down cost. Through reengineering, IBM improved on both dimensions.

IBM's is a success story. The company came from being in the red with an $8.1 billion loss in 1993 to net earnings of $6.3 billion in 1998.

Key Lessons

Given IBM's size and the wide scope of its Business Transformation initiative, its experience provides significant material for any other organization either going through or considering reengineering. What IBM set out to accomplish was ambitious, but what it achieved exceeded even its own expectations. Business Transformation lives up to its name—it truly represents fundamental change. Fortunately, Big Blue was able to discover a recipe for success and reorient itself to the market. When it comes to reengineering, others stand to learn from IBM's experience:

- *Well-understood need for change.* IBM was the grand American symbol of high tech, but that was all called into question when the company posted that $8 billion loss. Once considered an enviable place to work because of its benefits and promising future, IBM laid off thousands. Everyone agreed that change was necessary. Shrinking market share, growing customer dissatisfaction, and technology that was beginning to slip behind were problems recognized both inside and outside the company. Only radical change could save IBM.

- *Top executive sponsorship and responsibility.* Louis Gerstner has placed responsibility for Business Transformation success right at the top. The Corporate Executive Committee (CEC) owns all reengineering activities. Any issues or obstacles the Business Transformation project teams experience float to the top of the organization, and the CEC resolves them quickly.

- *Measurable results and rewards based on those results.* Every IBM employee, and in particular the CEC, has a large portion of their compensation based on their own performance, that of their business unit, and that of the overall company. Business Transformation means that a much larger portion of an individual's compensation is based on how the company performs as a whole. The new reward structure removes the incentive for building up one product line, geography, or business unit over another.

- *Customer-focused view of the business.* An IBM executive lamented, "We used to have dozens of salespeople calling on all sorts of people within the [customer's] organization selling bits and pieces." IBM has since adopted a "systems" approach to selling. A significant IBM core competency is its ability to provide a complete solution to its customers, including hardware, software, support, and implementation assistance. Fewer people are calling on the customer, but the customer relationship managers who do are responsible for seeing that IBM brings to bear the appropriate resources at the appropriate time to solve the customer's problems. IBM reorganized its processes, organization, and focus around the customer. It not only discovered cost savings as a result, but also improved satisfaction as customers consumed more IBM products and services.

- *Communication, integration, and cooperation among business units and divisions.* IBM struggled with the dilemma of whether to break the company into smaller, independent businesses or to keep it together as one large enterprise. In essence, the company had been operated in a separated fashion for many years. The conclusion was that IBM offered the customer unique value as a single source for a wide range of services, hardware, and software. IBM decided to leverage its size in new ways through Business Transformation. Key to IBM's current success is its ability to share knowledge and expertise across the organization. Through its new structure, IBM can deliver the right resources and the right solutions quickly. IBM is a seamless, coordinated organization as it rises to new challenges.

- *Simplification and globalization of processes.* Early on, IBM began its business transformation by just simplifying each process. This low-tech, unsophisticated exercise yielded savings very quickly. "We just accomplished things with less handoffs and less steps," says one executive. IBM had evolved into an organization with a number of different ways to accomplish any task. Part of the exercise simply involved "taking a look at all the ways we performed a process across the company, and picking one." The process the company chose for global consolidation was not necessarily a best practice standard in industry. Getting processes to happen more easily, quickly, and cheaply was the primary concern early on; then IBM tried to handle processes the same way across the globe. Company representatives emphasized that the benefits from merely simplifying any given process were immense.

- *It never ends.* IBM sees no concrete end in sight for its Business Transformation initiative. "We continuously find ways to improve. We just keep getting better," commented a senior IBM employee. The company has found that much of its effort now involves the entire user base and IBM community and is aware that room always exists to improve and become more efficient. New enhancements and best practices are shared throughout the organization. While realizing that the competition is obviously not going to go away, IBM continues to use what it learned from its reengineering experience to evolve and innovate.

IBM is one of the all-time great turnarounds. Who would have thought a company that is so huge and had such a conservative culture could so quickly come back from a multibillion-dollar loss? IBM's efforts in business transformation are an example of leadership, conviction, and the courage to change.

Universal Financial Corporation

Company Name:	
Universal Financial Corporation	
Project Name:	
"Reengineering to Tailor Customer Service"	

Functional Areas Covered:	Financial Performance
• **Private banking (PB)**	We don't provide the measures of financial performance for two reasons:
Savings:	(a) to preserve the anonymity of the corporation
• **Substantial savings as measured by both financial and nonfinancial metrics.**	(b) since PB is a relatively small portion of the corporation's total services, studying the effect of BPR on earnings and stock performance figures may not be appropriate.

Key Strengths:	Obstacles:
• **Not exclusively focused on cost-cutting**	• **Limited scope**
• **Education and training across the organization**	• **Lacked a compelling reason to force change**
• **Customer focus**	
• **Eliminated handoffs and placed authority at the front line**	

Comment:
"Reengineering was an investment to grow top-line revenues. The amazing growth, which exceeded our wildest dreams, is evidence of success. The customer had clearly approved of what we had done."

History and Background

Within Universal Financial Corporation (UFC), as in most financial service firms, private banking (PB) is the part of the organization that deals with high-net-worth individuals. Services provided through PB typically included brokerage services in mutual funds, bonds, options, and equity offerings as well as other fiduciary services and liquidity management. The PB market is a fragmented one, made up of numerous individuals worldwide. These wealthy clients became acutely aware of their investments' performance and risk exposure when the market surged in the early part of the nineties. The good news for UFC was that the PB business had been growing at greater than 20 percent annually. The bad news was that this motivated others to enter the industry and introduce more competition. UFC's competition had recognized that PB was highly profitable, a fact that spurred innovation while creating pressure to lower prices. The number and magnitude of offerings, along with improvements in service, changed UFC's environment at a dizzying pace.

Origins of the Problem/Recognition of the Opportunity

Competition is one of the first words across the lips of anyone describing the financial services industry. There was a lot to win or lose in the PB market. Given the high stakes, Universal Financial Corporation was committed to serving these lucrative clients. The company broadened its range of investment alternatives to generate high returns with reasonable risk exposure for its clients. With an established tradition of putting forth extra effort to help clients succeed with their investments, UFC enjoyed an excellent reputation in the PB marketplace.

Markets soared to new highs as competition within the industry heated up. UFC had long considered customer service a key differentiator, but the company's lead on the competition was shrinking. UFC wanted to improve its market position, not defend itself from innovative smaller players entering the market. Looking for new direction, the company conducted a survey of its private banking market that revealed:

- Two out of three respondents said, "I would like just one person who could help me with savings, investment, and credit needs."

- Nearly 60 percent of respondents said, "I would prefer to do all of my financial business at one institution that can bring together specialists and services I need rather than using several institutions or specialists."

UFC decided to target the market through customer intimacy. With a renewed mandate, UFC set out to win. The company was prepared to make large investments to bring not only more but better service to its clients. It was prepared to make large investments and to apply its capabilities globally. With its market becoming increasingly tough, UFC decided the best defense was a strong offense.

As UFC struggled to regroup in light of new dynamics in the marketplace, the company realized that its PB organization was neither truly integrated nor "client-aligned." The PB business had become more about products than customers. Under this structure, a single client spoke to multiple service administrators and staff assistants. With so many hands touching an account, the results were often inconsistent. Processes were complex and involved many different systems, and managing in this environment was impossible, because data were generally unavailable and information difficult to interpret. UFC recognized many of its internal shortcomings when it attempted to introduce innovative products that incorporated new levels of complexity. Without adequate supporting technology, manual intervention was required, but this introduced inaccuracies and other errors into the process. PB, by its nature focused on a limited market of wealthy individuals, had difficulty justifying large investments in technology based on the number of transactions and the number of service administrators involved.

Implementation Issues

UFC was committed to reengineering PB. The company made the investment up front, in talent, training, and systems, to ensure the project's success. Among the companies we examined, UFC's experience is unique. The focus from the outset was on the customer, although the result—improved service and therefore greater loyalty—is difficult to measure through an income statement.

While others invoke reengineering in their scramble for survival, UFC uses reengineering to solidify its market position. This company shows that reengineering is the philosophy of improvement. Not merely synonymous with cutting jobs or making more products cheaply, reengineering is about making businesses better.

3

Organization

Organizational design was a fundamental initial step in UFC's walk down the reengineering path. Most important, the company changed the way it addressed the market. In the new organization, clients had a single, familiar point of contact. Early on, the company's outside research led it to conclude that even best-practice customer service organizations are not necessarily "client intimate." New customer-focused positions fostered trust and had ultimate responsibility for seeing that the customer's needs were met—achieving customer intimacy. Teams were formed not around product, but around customer segments. The client-focused approach required UFC employees to become cross-trained and understand how all the pieces of the client's portfolio fit together. The company emphasized adequate training before implementation to ensure success. The impact on the organization was dramatic.

Culture

This is one of the most challenging areas for any organization, particularly a respected and successful one, to transform. UFC did not pursue a dramatic, overnight shift in its corporate culture. Instead, with a clear business goal before it, the company redesigned and changed its business one location, one product at a time. While many other advocates of reengineering insist on a "big bang" approach, UFC was in the enviable position of being able to err on the side of overstaffing, providing the company the extra resources required to reinvent the business while transactions were still going on. The upside was that the company did not undertake the project to lower its expense structure by cutting headcount and chopping costs.

On the other hand, unlike many of our case studies, UFC lacked a clear imperative to change. The threat to its business was more insidious and its approach to changing the company culture more evolutionary.

Key to its success in this area was hiring outside talent, an infusion of "new blood" that was not predisposed to perform tasks the same old way. In addition to this raw energy, the organization committed the best and brightest from its internal staff. This combination received visible, daily executive support. In some sense, the leadership of this group inspired the company as a whole.

The rest of the organization was able to understand and participate in the change through the project team's frequent and consistent communications. Generally, members of senior management sent these messages. As change pervaded the organization, the fear that usually accompanies it was conquered not only through communication but a dedication to training. Before implementation, those affected understood what was going to happen. They knew why it was happening, which allowed them to comfortably embrace the change the project brought.

Technology

It is nearly impossible to imagine any BPR effort without technology, but sometimes the pursuit of leading-edge information systems can become all-consuming. A number of reengineering initiatives later found themselves with nothing more than elaborate systems implementation. UFC was aware of these issues and spent a substantial amount of project time defining a manageable niche for technology use. One of the project's aims was to closely align the technology design with the business vision, organization, and process design.

To begin with, the company developed a road map that aided the process of managing multiple but interrelated projects. Breaking the project down into "chunks" and managing the design somewhat independently made it simpler to accomplish goals in each area and maintain the overall schedule.

Before adopting the reengineering initiative, the company established accelerated but disciplined methods for evaluating technology. The project was not overrun with consultants, but the company did obtain outside help in areas where focused roles had been defined. Not wanting to be too far out on a ledge by itself, UFC conducted a careful analysis of the software alternatives.

When it came to the technical aspects of its reengineering initiative, UFC established various mechanisms, such as a program management office, to track interdependencies and provided for dedicated cross-functional staffing on the team to ensure disciplined progress. By breaking the project down into manageable pieces and evaluating technology with outside sources, the company was able to maximize the return on its systems investment.

Processes

Following true reengineering methodology, UFC went "outside the box" and rethought every major PB servicing process. The company spent a short time analyzing its current environment (not wanting to get stuck in the past) and performed limited research on best practices. The team did draw upon some outside industry expertise.

Beginning with workshops involving all parties, both functional and technical, the team designed more efficient, powerful processes end-to-end. Every activity of the process was driven by business objectives rather than technical elegance, but the team also diligently captured the system requirements. After redesigning these processes, the project team asked a large percentage of stakeholders for their input. This final step also generated important buy-in.

Evaluation and Follow-up

UFC began the reengineering process by establishing a clear business vision and then articulating it through a three-year plan. The company sought outside input from market surveys, industry experts, and consultants. The rest of the process, from systems selection to process design, was aligned with the objectives that came out of this early step.

UFC defined success very differently from our other case-study companies. Initially the PB headcount increased as the business unit undertook reengineering. This gave UFC the breathing room to provide a consistent level of service to its sensitive customer base while rethinking the business. Customer service employees perform tasks very differently today in PB than before reengineering. They are now expected to be more customer-focused, which requires them to wear a number of functional hats. Employees have been appreciative of the openness the company has shown through its communication and investment in their training.

When all is said and done, customer service was improved, and the reengineering efforts helped lay the foundation for differentiating among clients. The company can see where it makes money and can better manage the process to offer customized service to its clients.

Clients who provide the greatest income to UFC now receive the highest levels of service. Those clients are the ultimate judge of reengineering's success.

Key Lessons

By following such a well-thought-out process and carefully documenting the results of the project, UFC now has some valuable insights about reengineering. The project team emphasized these key points:

- Establish a well-understood vision and objective to guide the project.

- Do not allow the scope of the project to expand.

- Show senior management's commitment and be willing to act to overcome project obstacles.

- Dedicate the right level of skills and resources to the project.

- Track progress against regular milestones and deadlines to generate the necessary momentum.

- Ensure strong coordination between teams.

- Communicate; too little communication can be deadly.

- Do not underestimate the silent pockets of resistance.

- Do not let technology dominate the solution; focus on the process before defining the systems.

- Be careful when technology lags too far behind other organizational changes.

- Do not spend too much time seeking the 110 percent solution; the project can settle for a 60 percent solution and get most of the way sooner (faster realization of benefits).

- Do not underestimate the complexity of reengineering and the business issues that must be dealt with.

Reengineering began with really thinking about what the business should be. UFC realized that customer service was key as a business strategy to position itself against the competition; reengineering enabled it to target its market with an integrated approach. The way the company addressed its clients profoundly changed as a result. Clients now receive proactive services from a single point of entry. UFC is more responsive, offers a broader spectrum of services, and is more flexible and adaptable because it conducts business differently.

Midwest Utility Corporation

Company Name: **Midwest Utility Corporation**		Ticker: N/A
Project Name: N/A		

Functional Areas Covered: • Distribution • Billing • Customer service	*Financial Performance* We don't provide financial measures to preserve the company's anonymity.
Savings: • Increased productivity • Improved customer service	

Key Strengths: • Recognized the changing marketplace in the wake of deregulation • Well-defined performance metrics	Obstacles: • Initiative was made up of a number of smaller uncoordinated efforts • Front-line employees did not buy in

Comment:
"It didn't get us to where we wanted to go, although we moved in the right direction. It was incredibly hard to muster the momentum to keep going."

History and Background

Midwest Utility came into being in the early 1940s. The company then shed unrelated businesses to focus on energy. As the communities it served grew, Midwest Utility built up its productive capacity with additional plants, and in 1964 the company teamed with 11 other utilities in 10 states to form the Mid-American Interpool Network, an interconnected electric distribution system. As the country faced the oil crisis of the seventies, the company added natural gas capabilities while exploring nuclear power production. Since then, the company has taken its operation global—including China, Colombia, Honduras, Jamaica, Pakistan, Peru, and the United Kingdom.

Origins of the Problem/Recognition of the Opportunity

Deregulation represents the most fundamental shift in the rules the industry has ever experienced. Midwest Utility understands the difficulties before it, and it is reengineering not only to overcome these obstacles but to dominate the industry.

Implementation Issues

Midwest Utility recognized that reengineering could not be a sideline initiative performed on some back-office function with little noticeable impact on the business. Reengineering was meant to be the rudder to steer the business in a new strategic direction.

Organization
Midwest Utility recognized that reorganization would be key to achieving the kind of performance required to compete in a deregulated market. The company created subsidiaries to operate in segments of the industry that adopted deregulation relatively quickly. One subsidiary focused on the production of power. Since its inception, this subsidiary has become involved in a consortium of power plants from around the world, including underserved markets such as South America and Asia.

A second subsidiary was created to market power. It focuses on buying and selling electricity, natural gas, and value-added services. By creating these smaller, focused organizations, Midwest Utility has accelerated change, and competitiveness in these areas has improved dramatically.

Culture

A long history of cost-plus pricing had left Midwest Utility with an environment in which change was foreign. Given that all expenses served as a basis to which a profit percentage was applied, there was not a strong motivation to improve productivity. Thanks to captive markets, Midwest took a low-risk approach to building and designing facilities, and the markets had no choice but to bear the burden of any costs that it passed along.

Midwest Utility spread the idea among its employees of becoming "Competitive by Year 2000." It was an attempt to bring a competitive spirit to the workforce, to infuse the company with the will to improve efficiency while raising the standard of customer service. Admittedly, changing Midwest Utility's culture has been a slow and difficult process.

Technology

In most areas of the company, technology systems did not undergo major changes. One area that did adopt new systems during the reengineering initiative was the billing and customer service area. In this instance, improvements in the supporting systems yielded an enormous benefit in conjunction with reengineering. A reengineered customer service cycle leveraged the new systems' ability to provide much richer details about the customer base. The system also gave Midwest Utility the ability to bill customers on behalf of a competitor, which had positive ramifications for the company in a deregulated environment. Midwest Utility's novel approach in this area is now considered a model for the industry. The company has some other technology advantages as well, such as a sophisticated power outage system, truck-mounted computers for order entry, global positioning and crew dispatching, and remote system dispatching capabilities.

Processes

Reengineering touched every major function within Midwest Utility. In almost every case, the initiative improved performance. Material handling, accounts payable, human resources, and even electric distribution can point to increases in efficiency. Unfortunately, these improvements did not reach the goals the organization set for itself in every case. It is important to recognize that the goals of the various constituencies were not the same—management wanted to lower costs by lowering headcount, the consultants wanted to achieve a dramatic strategic shift, and the employees wanted to maintain the status quo. These contradictory forces made progress along any dimension slow and difficult.

In finance and human resources, for example, management cut headcount to achieve its benchmarks before it finished reengineering processes. The result was lower headcount, but some of those employees were experienced people that the company needed to help transform the department. The company tried to minimize the impact of the cutbacks by placing unassigned employees in a temporary pool to give them an opportunity to find jobs in other parts of the company. However, employees did not perceive this and other efforts positively. Employees who remained were left with the same job and fewer resources, and on top of it all, these were the same people who were supposed to implement reengineering. They worked too hard and became too unhappy to be open to any vision of the future. In general, the result was lessened trust in management and a belief that reengineering would only cost jobs.

An evaluation of this experience reveals that the reengineering initiative in Midwest Utility was focused more on the steps than on the overall strategic initiative. In effect, BPR became a tool for cost savings achieved by headcount reductions rather than a way of reaching long-term goals. This said, it should be admitted that reengineering in the wake of a major structural change like deregulation is difficult at best and impossible at the worst. It is extremely difficult to formulate a vision when facing the wide-ranging changes that typically accompany deregulation. Thus, the experience of Midwest Utility is not unusual under these circumstances.

Evaluation and Follow-up

Reengineering did achieve some good at Midwest Utility. The company has a better handle on the cost of providing electricity, most functions are more efficient, and it is better positioned for deregulation. These benefits came at a cost, however. The organization still suffers from the scars of laying off so many employees; there is a lack of complete support for management initiatives that will negatively affect the organization's ability to change in the future. Furthermore, the initiative took a long time and has yet to be completed. From a return on investment perspective, it is uncertain that Midwest Utility's reengineering experience produced positive returns. As time goes on, the company hopes that the recurring benefits from reengineering will outweigh its investment, even with all its related costs.

Key Lessons

- *Vision.* In the case of Midwest Utility, one critical element that seemed to be missing from the reengineering mix was vision. It is difficult, if not impossible, to convince anyone that any trip is worth the effort if the destination is unknown. Reengineering is a very long journey, especially for an organization unfamiliar with change, and the destination must be communicated to and accepted by everyone as the right place to go. The vision must be something the whole organization can get behind.

- *Commitment from the top.* Given the length of time and the level of effort it takes to reengineer, an organization's leadership needs to remain steadfastly behind the initiative. Lacking a clear vision, Midwest Utility's management was unable to maintain its conviction that reengineering was the right thing to do. In one case, there was some debate concerning the centralization versus decentralization of distribution facilities. Wavering made any change difficult to implement. Reengineering has to be seen as something that will happen, not something that might happen.

- *Reengineering amid industry-wide change.* Some debate remains about whether the appropriate response to an industry shift, such as deregulation, is to improve current operations or to reengineer to create dramatically different operations. Obviously, the jury is still out on that question. Reengineering often requires significant introspection for a firm. For Midwest Utility, this soul-searching should have led the company to conclude it needed to focus more on customers and producers because of deregulation. According to Hammer and Champy (1993), all too often reengineering involves exhaustively defining the "as-is" mechanics of a business. Instead, the prescribed reengineering method should be focused on aligning the operations with the company's emergent competitive strategy. Reengineering and deregulation should not compete but converge, because more than ever the company must focus on revenues and cost drivers.

- *Beware of effects on employee morale.* Reengineering as a method for improving an organization's performance has lost considerable public favor. No doubt this is largely due to its association with layoffs, headcount reduction, outsourcing, and other actions taken in its name. At Midwest Utility, there had been little change and no layoffs for decades. Suddenly, management declared a change under the title of reengineering, and some jobs were lost. In the absence of a vision of where the company was headed, this initiative was bound to have problems. But such a "shock" also prepares employees for change in the future, and it is hoped that the changes will benefit Midwest Utility.

Baxter International, Inc.

Company Name:	Ticker:
Baxter International, Inc.	NYSE: BAX

Project Name:
N/A

Functional Areas Covered:
- All areas of the company were included

Savings:
- Quadrupled the stock price
- Improved productivity
- Reduced development cycle time
- Doubled return on equity

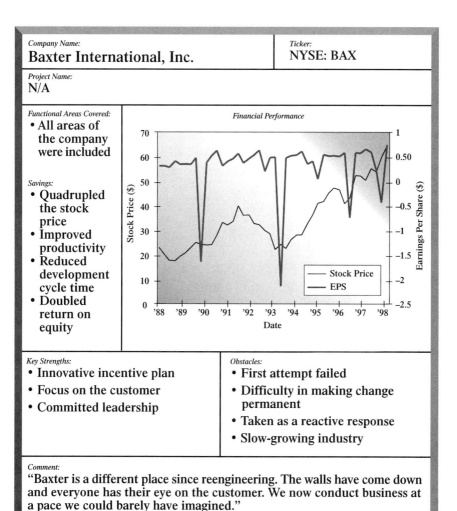

Financial Performance

Key Strengths:
- Innovative incentive plan
- Focus on the customer
- Committed leadership

Obstacles:
- First attempt failed
- Difficulty in making change permanent
- Taken as a reactive response
- Slow-growing industry

Comment:
"Baxter is a different place since reengineering. The walls have come down and everyone has their eye on the customer. We now conduct business at a pace we could barely have imagined."

History and Background

B axter began as the Don Baxter Intravenous Products Corporation, named after a California physician, to distribute intravenous solutions made in Los Angeles. In 1939 Baxter research and development produced the first sterilized vacuum-type blood device.

Origins of the Problem/Recognition of the Opportunity

Baxter, like the rest of the medical supply industry, found itself in crisis in the early nineties. The old environment in which the company operated had changed: Competition intensified, regulations became more stringent, and health maintenance organizations dominated the scene. In this context, research and development expenses moved skyward as the costs of the processes and technology employed took a bigger bite out of the bottom line. Prices were forced down, and costs were climbing. Growth rates and returns shrank. A critical problem was that the company was no longer producing enough cash flow from operations to support its historical dividend policy. The result was a slow liquidation of capital in the business. The hallmark event was the stock price's fall from the mid-forties to the low twenties—a clear signal that the company was in danger.

Implementation Issues

Harry Kraemer, the current president and CEO of Baxter, remembers that difficult time in its history. He admits that initial attempts at reengineering the firm could be described as only mediocre. "I think it is human nature to believe that bad situations are only temporary. We lacked real objectivity about our situation," he recalls. Initial reengineering efforts never took hold. Kraemer remembers that the organization lacked the change in mindset required for success. But even with this less than impressive start, the company discovered a key that made its later initiatives work.

Organization

Before reengineering, Baxter had some 300-plus performance metrics. Obviously, people could use any one of these to point to improvements in performance. And reward systems were not aligned with the company's overall interests. For example, maximizing the divisional income statement caused working capital to increase. Net income was maximized at the expense of higher inventory and a greater number of day's sales outstanding. Baxter was getting the results it was rewarding, but it was getting the right answers to the wrong questions.

The key to making reengineering activities work for Baxter was incentives. Baxter called the initiative the "Shared Investment Program," or SIP. The plan involved the top 72 people in the organization taking loans, which were guaranteed by the company through a local bank, and investing the proceeds in the company's stock. If the company performed well and the stock price rose, so did the fortunes of these influential managers and executives. The average loan size was approximately $2 million. Suddenly, "we had some serious skin in the game," remembers Kraemer. These top managers and executives had every incentive to understand what was negatively affecting their stock price and correct it. The SIP created a lot of instant learning.

Behaviors changed, and employees started asking new questions. Before reengineering, each executive at a management meeting presented his or her plans to the committee, and usually only the CEO and CFO asked questions. The understanding among the group members was, "Don't rain on my parade and I won't rain on yours."

The SIP program transformed the meetings. Instead of being confronted only by the top executives, managers were grilled by a whole group of experts—each other. Most surprising was the cooperation that grew out of these meetings. Often, departments shared resources as they looked for ways to get the same results at a lower cost. They all knew what additional profit percentage was worth, and how improved cash flow would affect the share price and hence their wealth. Once committed to capital expenditure targets and research and development budgets, they forced one another to make sure that the columns labeled headcount and dollars invested added up to 100 percent. This situation created the sense of urgency the company was looking for.

These managers became expert at prioritizing and allocating resources for the entire company. They acted like owners themselves, because now they were.

Culture

One manager stated that before reengineering he felt "[he] would rather be lucky than good." The comment embodies the general helplessness that many felt. It was as if some strange paralysis had fallen upon the company. How could any individual really affect such a large and complex organization? On the other hand, most also believed the company was never going away.

At the root of this belief was the perception that the situation was only temporary. Initial headcount reductions in an attempt to lower costs resulted only in simple work-flow changes. "We laid off one or two people from every department and redistributed the work among the remaining," remembered one manager. People thought that if they could only work harder, they would get through this crisis. Objectivity was clouded as employees pointed to Baxter's history of success. In the beginning, they treated the situation like an aberration.

These initial responses did not work. Over time, departments added back the one or two people they had lost, reasoning it would not really harm the company overall. It became clear that unless it adopted another course of action, the company would continue to drift.

"The longer you're around, the harder it is to take on change," recounted Harry Kraemer. "There were a number of us who committed ourselves to thinking through it." The SIP went a long way toward producing the correct response to Baxter's situation. The company began its reengineering initiatives anew. This time around, reengineering amounted to what has been described as the "Manhattan Project." In addition to assigning the most talented people to the initiative, most executives and top managers ended up spending a majority of their time guiding the reinvention of Baxter. With a simple message (described in the process section) and a clear sense of purpose, the company committed itself to change.

Technology

Unlike many other examples of reengineering, Baxter did not focus on implementing new systems or adopting complex technology. Rather, it used the tools it already had more effectively. Through reengineering, the company began to more effectively share resources, including systems, across the organization. Baxter used its corporate building blocks, including its people and systems, in a whole new way.

Processes

Baxter's reengineering focused on taking every process and changing its orientation along the following dimensions:

- *Improve communications.* Simply put, many of the classic hand-offs between departments or functions resulted in inefficiencies, largely owing to lack of communication. It became imperative to coordinate the process of communication, with each party understanding what role it was to play and why.

- *Focus externally.* Although less than 2 percent of the workforce ever comes in contact with the customer, the organization had to become customer-oriented. For every process, management asked, "Does the customer want our product?" A push took place to make Baxter appear seamless to its customer, not a slew of disjointed departments.

- *Generate value for the shareholders.* This objective simplified the business. From 300 different metrics to the definitive, timely, no-calculation-required measure, Baxter had an easy way to compare itself with others in the market. The measure was a variation of the free cash-flow metric, wherein additional investment was netted out of operating cash flows for the period. This measure was calculated at the end of every month. It was simple, easy to grasp, and directly relevant to the stock price. The act of re-designing the business became deliberate, with share price as the yardstick.

Applying these three easy principles produced the results the company was looking for. Baxter found through reengineering that the company could do better than the sum of the individual optimized units. The company was able to use coordinated operations to discover new, profitable growth and significantly improve its cash flow. The market has proved that Baxter's efforts have indeed added value to the shareholders—the stock price more than quadrupled since reengineering began. Baxter demonstrates the power of correctly linking rewards with the organization's strategy. Focusing on the customer and getting the entire company pulling in the same direction produced results.

Pfizer, Inc.

Company Name: **Pfizer, Inc.**	Ticker: NYSE: PFE

Project Name:
Winds of Change

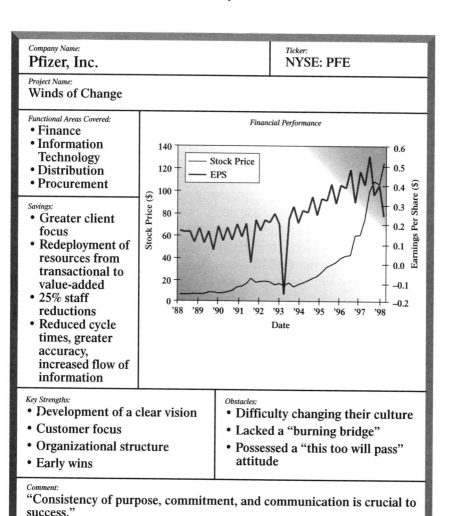

Functional Areas Covered:
- Finance
- Information Technology
- Distribution
- Procurement

Savings:
- Greater client focus
- Redeployment of resources from transactional to value-added
- 25% staff reductions
- Reduced cycle times, greater accuracy, increased flow of information

Financial Performance

Key Strengths:
- Development of a clear vision
- Customer focus
- Organizational structure
- Early wins

Obstacles:
- Difficulty changing their culture
- Lacked a "burning bridge"
- Possessed a "this too will pass" attitude

Comment:
"Consistency of purpose, commitment, and communication is crucial to success."

3

History and Background

Pfizer is one of the world's leading research-based pharmaceutical companies. The firm discovers, develops, manufactures, markets, and sells pharmaceuticals (prescription and over-the-counter) for humans and animals. The company was founded in 1849 by two German immigrants—Charles Pfizer and his cousin Charles Erhart. Pfizer's focus for much of its first hundred years was specialty chemicals. Its transition to pharmaceuticals began with the mass-production of penicillin during World War II.

In the interest of capitalizing on its core competencies, the company's business portfolio underwent a significant transition over the course of the nineties. Nonpharmaceutical businesses—chemicals, cosmetics, minerals, and medical devices—were divested. Significant internal and external investments were made during this period consistent with the firm's focus on pharmaceuticals. This is demonstrated by research and development (R&D) growth of 18 percent over the decade. Pfizer's 1998 R&D expenditures of $2.3 billion exceeded those of any other U.S.-based pharmaceutical company. Leading products stemming from Pfizer's R&D include Norvasc (hypertension), Zoloft (depression), Zithromax (antibiotic), Diflucan (fungal disease), and Viagra (male erectile dysfunction). Each of these therapeutics is either the first or second largest selling product in its category. Consistent with its strategic imperative to be the "partner of choice," Pfizer augments its internal efforts with a wide array of third-party collaborations.

Origins of the Problem/Recognition of the Opportunity

The pharmaceutical industry's operating environment in the early nineties was fragmented. New technologies were significantly increasing the productivity as well as the therapeutic scope of research and development. Societal changes such as the "graying" of the population in many developed countries, patients' more active management of their own health care, the erosion of stigmas associated with certain diseases like depression, and the AIDS crisis were some of the factors resulting in increased demand not just for pharmaceuticals, but for health care in general. These demands were met with various cost-containment initiatives. Payers such as employers, insurance companies, governments, and patients themselves initiated or supported measures such as generic substitution, managed care, restricted access, and making products ineligible for reimbursement.

Pfizer, despite a very robust pipeline of "best in class" therapeutics, was faced with a very uncertain operating environment. Industry responses included diversification, a moderation in the level of commitment to R&D, and vertical and horizontal integration. Pfizer's response was to *increase* its commitment to innovation. This strategy reflected its belief that the industry was far from mature. Many opportunities to improve the safety and efficacy of current treatments existed. In addition, there were many diseases for which no effective therapy was available.

Although Pfizer never deviated from its commitment to innovation, it was clear the risk attendant on that strategy was increasing. The intent behind business process reengineering was to reduce this risk. Eliminating non-value-added activities and reengineering processes allowed the company to redeploy savings in the mainstream business and heighten the productivity of various parts of the organization by providing better quality service.

Implementation

The initiative was led by Pfizer's chief financial officer. A steering committee representing each functional area (finance, information technology, distribution, and procurement) provided technical and managerial oversight. Individuals from various organizations were assigned to the project on a full-time basis to document existing processes, conduct client interviews, benchmark, and develop recommendations. External consulting resources also played a key role in facilitating the initiative.

One of the first goals of the project's leadership was to establish a clear sense of purpose and mission. A clear and compelling vision can inspire, motivate, and galvanize an organization toward common behaviors and goals. After much discussion and debate, a vision emerged. A key feature of the vision was its tight linkage to the goals of the company. The purpose and mission are outlined below.

Purpose

Pfizer's discovery, development, and commercialization of advances in health care serve all of the company's stakeholders, including employees, investors, and patients. The purpose of the support functions is to foster this objective by providing the highest caliber financial, strategic, and operational support to all its constituencies.

Mission

The mission is to address the strategic imperatives of Pfizer, Inc., by

- improving the company's ability to *respond to the emerging marketplace* by providing state-of-the-art financial, information, and operational resources;

- *enhancing shareholder value* by implementing practices that foster strategic thinking and decision making and by effectively managing the company's financial resources;

- heightening *speed* in all facets of the business: decision making, dissemination of information, and business processes;

- lowering the company's *cost structure* by operating more efficiently while continuously improving the quality of services; and

- continually investing in its most important asset: its *employees*.

The vision served as the guidepost for the entire initiative and was continually communicated to employees. The rallying cry "On the Path to Preeminence" was coined to capture the essence of the vision.

Outcomes

Some of the major outcomes, consistent with the goal of addressing the strategic imperatives of Pfizer, Inc., are summarized below.

Responding to the Emerging Marketplace

The extensive redesign, development, and installation of a new suite of operational and financial systems provided more timely, comprehensive, accessible, and consistent information. The new revenue cycle system, for example, made customer information more immediate and complete. Order, invoice, and payment processing became more responsive to increasing customer demands for electronic data interchange.

The consolidation and reconfiguration of the U.S. distribution infrastructure reduced the number of facilities from six to three. New state-of-the-art logistics centers provided significant flexibility for changes in volume, customer base, and product mix. Order cycle times were reduced from five, six, or seven days to three or four days. Significant costs savings were realized as well.

Enhancing Shareholder Value

Process reengineering afforded Pfizer the opportunity to redeploy resources to value-added activities, such as tax and treasury planning. Reducing risks associated with foreign exchange, interest rates, and income taxes received heightened focus.

The format, focus, and timeliness of financial information used to foster management's strategic decision making were completely revised. The emphasis of monthly financial reviews with the chairman and other top executives shifted from discussions of what had happened to expectations and plans of action. The monthly financial report changed from a static, internally focused document to one featuring external benchmarks, forecasts, and expectations. In addition, the company changed management reporting policies to heighten the linkage between results and responsibility.

Speed

The preparation time for the federal tax return was reduced by four months, allowing the company to redeploy two staff years in support of tax planning.

Outsourcing the savings and investment plan enabled employees to gain information on the status of their accounts or make certain transactions almost 24 hours a day, instead of being able to do so only during business hours.

Revised work processes enabled the internal audit group to spend approximately two weeks preparing field audits instead of 14 weeks. As a result, key audit findings were communicated faster.

Cost Structure

Reengineering activities collectively enabled the company to reduce its level of support by 25 percent, or 300 people. This figure understates how much efficiency Pfizer gained by redeploying resources to value-added activities.

- The company increased its use of shared services in finance for various transactional activities, such as payroll, accounts payable, general ledger, capital assets, and so on. In Europe, for example, the number of financial organizations serving the major markets was reduced from 33 to 6. This initiative also resulted in more consistent policies and procedures company-wide.

- The purchasing organization's charter changed from tactical (routine purchasing activities such as order specifications) to strategic. The new focus includes forming strategic supply teams and strategic alliances with key suppliers, and leveraging cross-divisional and global purchases. In addition to substantive savings, numerous quality dimensions improved.

Employees

Although change created uncertainty and anxiety, the company clearly recognized the importance of improving the capabilities and work environment of its most important asset—employees.

- Efforts to enhance employees' skills included adopting a comprehensive performance management process. Pfizer increased its emphasis on formal training as well as managers' responsibility to teach and mentor. The organization promoted rotational assignments to provide employees with diverse experiences.

- Given the new skills required, the company took steps to enhance processes pertaining to organizational needs assessment, sourcing talent, and recruitment and selection.

- Pfizer instituted numerous programs to foster cultural change. Communications emphasized the importance of the "pathways to preeminence," namely customer focus, continuous improvement, enterprise, and teamwork. Expert speakers, town meetings, and off-site team-building exercises were also employed.

Key Lessons

- *The role of vision.* Again, vision plays an important role in emphasizing the initiative's purpose and mission.

- *Importance of clear and constant communications.* Change is extremely unsettling to people. Management must continually communicate what is unfolding and why. The difficulty in Pfizer's case was compounded by the fact that the company was doing well and its future prospects were excellent. The message to employees was that the company had to change ahead of the curve. This would enable Pfizer to avoid some of the devastating consequences that befell other industries and companies. Even if it is difficult news, tell people what you know when you know it.

- *Cultural impact.* The existing culture was an enormous challenge. The reengineering effort required risk taking, challenging the status quo, "blank sheet of paper thinking," and so forth. The company was accustomed to gradual change. The new environment demanded that people own their jobs and be entrepreneurial. The old culture was a command-and-control management style. In addition, employees frequently referred to the "Pfizer family." It had been somewhat of a "job for life" atmosphere. The goal was to move to more of a meritocracy—the company had responsibilities on behalf of its employees, but employees also had a responsibility on behalf of the company. A consistent message and walking the talk are critical.

Cultural change under any circumstance, however, is a lengthy process. At Pfizer, there was a strong belief that the company had no real need to improve. The phrase "if it isn't broken, don't fix it" was heard regularly.

■ *Benchmarking.* Looking to the outside and seeing what was done in other organizations was extremely effective in demonstrating what was possible. Client interviews further highlighted the need to do things differently.

■ *Charter and process before organization and systems.* A common reengineering pitfall is automating current processes or dictating arbitrary cost savings or headcount reductions. Pfizer succeeded partly because it first evaluated functions' roles. Many things simply were unnecessary or needed to be refocused. Management considered a number of alternatives on how to best do the work. Once the charter and process have been established, it is appropriate to assess the supporting human resources and how technology can help the reengineering process succeed.

■ *Staying the course.* There is always a certain constituency that believes change will simply go away if one waits long enough. This can severely retard the pace of the initiative. The leadership of the Pfizer project made it clear that change *would* happen. This perception was reinforced by instituting a couple of quick but effective "wins." In addition, those who understood and participated in the new process were recognized and rewarded.

■ *Carefully measuring costs and benefits.* Tangible metrics foster accountability. But intangible benefits should not go unrecognized either. At Pfizer, people now feel better about their responsibilities, reports are available on a more timely basis, more information enhances decision making, and policies and procedures are uniform.

Pfizer's reengineering of the finance, information technology, distribution, and procurement functions exceeded some very bold goals. In addition to saving money, the changes better enabled the support functions to be business partners by helping the corporation address its strategic imperatives. In addition, significant cultural benefits accrued as the organization began to view change not as a threat but an opportunity.

Lessons Learned
from BPR Practices

What can we learn from our BPR surveys and interviews? While the experiences varied, there were some common themes that enabled us to distill some clear messages. This section provides a summary of the lessons learned from these experiences.

Do not reengineer unless you can justify
a need for dramatic change.

Companies should not attempt to reengineer unless they have a well-articulated and justified need. This is particularly important for employees, because to achieve buy-in for reengineering, management must be able to clearly show employees the large gap between the company's current condition and its future goals. One of our survey respondents is an excellent example. In this case, the vice president of operations arrived from an overseas location in which BPR efforts had been successful. Since costs had escalated, management brought him in to "fix" the operations. Interestingly, a TQM initiative was already in progress. But the newly imported vice-president of operations was not aware of employee resistance to initiatives such as TQM or BPR. The resistance from the union was fierce, and attempts to get them to agree with and without consultants were not fruitful. The relentless pursuit of BPR efforts nearly bankrupted the company. The division had to be sold and the vice president lost his job.

This case illustrates that it is very important to determine the need for reengineering through careful analysis. Since BPR may have negative connotations to employees, other management initiatives may be more suitable. In fact, written comments on our surveys indicated that management frequently implemented BPR programs, with limited success, because the CEO was fascinated by the notion. Embracing BPR because it is in fashion will undoubtedly lead to failure, because the road to success in reengineering is a perilous one.

Ensure the total commitment of senior management.

Total commitment from senior management is crucial for success, as Pfizer's experience demonstrates. Partly because of competition from other drug companies and partly due to the pending expiry of patents, Pfizer felt the need to change employee attitudes toward innovation. The interesting feature of this case was that the rewards of BPR efforts were not immediately obvious to either the employees or the management. But the title of the BPR effort, "Winds of Change," reflected the benefits the company expected to achieve. The purpose of the BPR effort was to get employees ready for change in the coming years. Clearly, an effort with such an amorphous objective is not likely to succeed without unswerving commitment from the top. In Pfizer's case, this commitment was present, and the entire initiative was very successful.

Such commitment, especially in the absence of a tangible goal, such as reducing cycle time in a process, is crucial for success. The charisma of the leader can rally the forces behind this difficult journey. The analogy in Hammer and Stanton (1995) is that of Moses leading the Israelites to the Promised Land. When the journey began, Moses' followers saw in front of them miles and miles of endless sand. Yet they agreed to follow him, because he was the magnet. Similarly, the leader of the BPR effort should have a vision, and BPR should be used to communicate that vision to the employees. Examples include George Fisher of Kodak, Louis Gerstner of IBM, Larry Bossidy of Allied Signal, Jack Welch of GE, and Harry Kraemer of Baxter International.

Provide a vision for your team members.

The path to success in BPR is a difficult one, so it is important to clearly outline the rewards for employees' efforts. Without this, employees are likely to focus on the difficulties of BPR rather than the rewards. This happened to Midwest Utility. Because of the deregulation initiative from the Energy Policy Act of 1992, Midwest Utility began facing competition for its wholesale market and eventually for the retail market as well. This competition was the trigger for the BPR effort, but management seemed to be greatly concerned about reducing costs rather quickly, and it did not offer employees a vision of success and rewards. This was partly due to the uncertainty associated with the energy market. For example, it was unclear whether the costs of the nuclear power plants would be recovered in the rates after the arrival of competition, an issue primarily in the hands of the rate commission and the state legislators. But the employees saw only headcount reduction and the accompanying loss of morale. Thus, management could not get the employees to journey with them to the Promised Land, because its existence, let alone the path to it, was in question.

The issue is merely a question of risk and reward. If the employees are willing to risk undertaking BPR, then they should be rewarded immediately or told when and how much reward to expect. Otherwise, BPR may not succeed.

Consultants should not take over the BPR project. Let the BPR team run the project.

It is important to use consultants effectively in any BPR exercise. They should be used to objectively analyze the situation and also to bring in experience from implementing BPR in other situations. Remember, however, that no one knows an organization's processes and how they are linked together better than the employees. Thus, it is far better to empower the employees than to have consultants learn from them and then use the knowledge to improve the processes.

A multibillion-dollar enterprise that we interviewed found itself in a competitive environment and realized it was not making money on a replacement cost basis. In fact, it was losing money, partly because of price escalation on projects that took several years to complete. Consultants were brought in to change the strategic thrust and also to help on the bid-to-bill process. The operations and the bidding process were complex. The consultants started studying the process in depth and suggesting changes. The employees vehemently resisted the changes. At this point, the consultants took ownership of the BPR initiative and started implementing the changes. Transferring the ownership of the project to the consultants enraged the employees even further. Management was not happy with the results. The whole experience was unsatisfactory for everyone.

It is very important for the BPR team to retain control and ownership of the project and then transfer the benefits and energy of this drive to the employees, so they can pursue BPR goals on their own.

Communicate the purpose of BPR efforts effectively and obtain cooperation from the employees.

Communicating the goals of reengineering and also the efforts involved in accomplishing it is crucial to its success. If the employees are confused about the goals and what it takes to achieve them, the results will be disastrous. One of our sample firms, American Express, recognized this and communicated the need for cooperation well before the reengineering exercises began. The CFO of Pfizer also made a very conscious attempt to make employees understand the need for change.

IBM illustrates how clear communication from the top can foster success. Since becoming CEO, Louis Gerstner has traveled extensively to promote the goals of the BPR efforts. At some level, this becomes a matter of selling the idea to employees who may be reluctant to change, while keeping the communication lines open both ways.

Personal communication is also important to convey the importance of the BPR effort through tone of voice, facial expression, and body language as well as words. Here are some points to remember for effective communication:

1. *Simplify, simplify, and further simplify.* The goals and the process involved in successfully completing the BPR program need to be simplified as much as possible, because buy-in and understanding from employees is crucial to success.

2. *Keep the channels open, and keep them two-way.* Because BPR initiatives are both radical and wide-ranging, questions are likely to arise in the wake of these big changes. Therefore, it is very important to keep the channels of communication open throughout the process. In fact, depending on the extent of reengineering

(whether it is firm-wide or just a few processes), it might be advisable to hire a communication manager to help disseminate the goals and the steps involved in accomplishing them.

3. *Know your audience.* At all stages, treat the audience with respect and convey the information as honestly and clearly as possible.

4. *Link goals to corporate strategy.* An important reason for the success of reengineering among our respondents is the effectiveness with which the corporate goals were linked to the BPR efforts. Stay focused on the BPR goals, and keep your communications tied to them.

Ask such questions as these:

- "What are the mission-critical processes to be reengineered?"
- "How do we prioritize them?"
- "How do we sequence them?"

One of our respondents had difficulties because it did not link reengineering efforts to corporate strategy. The success of BPR efforts depended on the fortunes of the airline industry and also on the reduction of labor time in the different processes. The reengineering efforts were not clearly tied to the corporate strategy of making the firm the leader in manufacturing airline spare parts. Instead, the use of reengineering initiatives was ad-hoc and was begun because it was successful in a sister organization. Not surprisingly, reengineering failed. It is difficult to overemphasize the need to have a clear corporate strategy and to link the BPR efforts to it.

Motivate the employees.

As indicated earlier, the critical common thread in the success of several of our cases is the participation of the rank and file. Therefore, it is important to motivate the employees by explaining how they can share in the corporate success of the reengineering efforts. Baxter International found that employee incentives went a long way toward ensuring cooperation among different departments. Initially, the incentives were restricted to senior management, but these are now being extended to lower levels of management to increase buy-in.

The absence of incentives for employees to undertake this difficult but important initiative can lead to failure. Midwest Utility began reengineering in the wake of deregulation and found it difficult both to incent the employees and provide a vision of where reengineering would take them. Thus, employees resented BPR efforts and offered little cooperation, which led to a general lack of success.

Choose the appropriate metrics.

As IBM and Baxter International demonstrate, a proliferation of performance metrics can confuse employees and undermine the reengineering efforts. The characteristics of the right metrics include:

- Simplicity
- Relevance to the process being reengineered
- Relationship to the goal
- Parsimony (the fewer metrics, the better)

The success of employee efforts emerges in a variety of ways, some financial and some nonfinancial. Ultimately, all the metrics in the firm could be affected by the reengineering efforts. It is up to the reengineering team to decide which metrics to emphasize and also which ones the employees can affect immediately. These decisions should be well articulated to avoid confusion. Baxter International, at one point, had more than 300 performance metrics, and the CEO posed a simple question to the senior management: "Which of these metrics are directly related to shareholder value?" They settled on a variation of a measure of free cash flows and stopped emphasizing other measures as much. This helped employees determine exactly how their efforts related to the metric. The result was the well-known turnaround in Baxter International. IBM accomplished similar results with emphasis on the most important metrics.

Do not ignore the human element in BPR.

Reengineering has always been advanced as a "top-down" activity, but its success depends on how quickly and how effectively the employees embrace changes, such as new design and new technology. If the employees do not get involved in the reengineering process, they are less likely to embrace changes. While it may not be necessary to involve *all* the employees in BPR, it is folly to follow a strict top-down approach, which does not give the employees a sense of ownership. Successful managers know that heavy-handedness promotes ill-will and goes against what they have learned about motivating people.

At Baxter International, ownership and buy-in were guaranteed through a novel incentive scheme. In other organizations, such as Pfizer, employees formed teams that provided suggestions for improvement. Tapping employees' creative side is crucial to success.

Do's and Don'ts

Based on our interviews, we have distilled a list of do's and don'ts for reengineering:

DO

- Have commitment from senior management for the initiative
- Have clear reengineering goals
- Reengineer mission-critical processes
- Communicate your goals effectively to the employees
- Obtain buy-in from employees by involving them
- Reengineer when there is a clear need for radical change, even if the problems are not immediate
- Encourage and reward employee creativity
- Stay focused on the objectives

- Develop appropriate metrics
- Communicate these metrics to the parties involved
- Provide the right incentives and reward employees appropriately for success
- Encourage continuous improvements

DON'T

- Make half-hearted attempts at BPR
- Have unrealistic expectations
- Reengineer too many processes at the same time
- Ignore the politics involved in resistance to change
- Underestimate the power of incentives to elicit creativity
- Think that incentives need only be monetary
- Pursue too many ideas
- Have too many performance metrics
- Think that a BPR initiative is an end in itself

What's Going Wrong with Business Process Reengineering?

Over the past five years, the BPR paradigm has caught on throughout the United States and other parts of the world. Most major consulting enterprises today offer professional help on this topic, and several *Fortune* 500 corporations have embarked on some form of BPR implementation. Most of these companies have made a significant investment in consultants, training, software, hardware, and time. The number of seminars and conferences on the subject has grown exponentially.

But is BPR affecting the bottom line, as originally claimed? Having personally implemented several BPR initiatives in at least ten different companies, and having offered courses in the strategy, we have some concerns. At a recent private gathering of chief executives from midwestern manufacturing companies, less than 20 percent stated that their BPR efforts have paid off in terms of profitability by reducing costs and headcount and avoiding costs. Many say that BPR's role in performance measurement, such as balanced scorecard or long-term strategy, is more valuable than short-term cost cutting or headcount reduction, and cited culture shock and changing needs as the major problems.

We all understand and appreciate the theory behind the BPR concept and its immense power in unleashing the strategic information needed to manage our business in the long run. But those who have implemented BPR are sending signals of distress and confusion about its relevance. So, what went wrong with their efforts? Did they misunderstand? Is BPR another "flavor of the month"?

After talking to companies that either have implemented or are currently implementing BPR, analyzing the survey results in chapter 2, and reflecting on our own experiences, we found several things that may have contributed to their lackluster results. The following are the nine most common pitfalls.

Conducting a Superficial Analysis of Reengineering

Timing is crucial for initiating any new projects, instilling new ideas, or abolishing existing mindsets. In the past five years many companies have resorted to "program of the month (or year)" concepts to address some of their problems. Unfortunately, BPR has become a member of this club, along with ABC (activity-based costing), JIT (just-in-time manufacturing), TQM (total quality management), and others. Often, middle management has read about these new concepts or attended seminars or conferences. Upon returning to their offices, they instruct their subordinates to "do a BPR study." The decision to do that is often made on the spur of the moment while listening to success stories at conferences. We have seen a majority of conference attendees agreeing on the symptoms of poor processes, and they wholeheartedly accept the idea that their processes are crippling productivity and consuming valuable resources without adding much value.

The problem is that most managers do not attempt to further investigate the inefficiencies of their own processes and systems. BPR conferences address issues of cost, value-added, layers of management, continuous improvement, and performance measurement with the help of BPR analysis. They lead most companies to believe that BPR analysis is the "thing to do" and that it can cure most of the organization's ills. However, few companies want to spend any time diagnosing their problems in depth. They would much rather take a canned approach or solution and try to fit the problems into the solution.

Overall, business process reengineering is not yet well understood, although many papers have been published about its merits and the detailed process of implementing it. Published information on the actual results of implementing such new cost systems is very scanty.

Cooper (1989) has illustrated in great detail how to determine when a new cost system is needed. He argues that product cost distortions arise mainly from disproportionate resources some products consume compared with others. He recommends some classical litmus tests for companies to see if they have cost distortion problems and if BPR can help them. The tests include examination of overheads, product or stock keeping unit (SKU) proliferation, increasing design and process complexity, numerous customers with varying volumes, multiple distribution channels, and unusually high market shares, to name just a few. This study does not deal with these tests in any detail. We believe many companies have failed to understand such litmus tests properly, and without them, any BPR implementation will fail to deliver the promised results.

Lacking a Complete Strategic Picture

The Kellogg Graduate School of Management has been conducting executive education on BPR over the last six years. We have seen participation in these seminars from all levels of management—from the CEO to the CFO to the financial analyst and operational managers. The seminars started out with mostly senior executives who had heard about BPR and were curious about what it is and what it can do for them. We then saw middle-level executives attending our sessions, primarily at the direction of their superiors. They were there to calibrate BPR as a new world-class management tool and to determine whether their companies should adopt this technique to increase their market share, become more profitable, and maintain their sustainable competitive advantage.

Finally, we saw practitioners attending our seminars. Interestingly, what they heard in the seminar seemed to be different from what their bosses heard, although we consistently presented the same material! We came to believe that there was a huge perception gap among different levels of management about their own business. We have repeatedly seen that BPR practitioners were neither completely exposed to all facets of their business, nor did they entirely understand its strategic nature. In a large multinational, multidivisional, and multisite enterprise, we have seen BPR typically implemented in a single pilot site. It is not uncommon for the implementors to lack the big picture about the enterprise and how the product line, product cost/price, and process decisions that they make will affect the entire business.

Everyone has heard repeatedly how bad it is to proliferate the product lines (numerous SKUs). Without batting an eye, people point fingers at the marketing folks and blame them for all the complexities (manufacturing, purchasing, order processing, inventory holding costs, etc.) they have created. We have seen a study that estimated the cost of maintaining an additional part in a company's material resource planning system at $10,000! If the costs of processes and activities determine business decisions, every manufacturing company should theoretically make just one product (Henry Ford's "I will make any color Model T as long as it is black"), and every service company should provide only one service! We don't live in such a world any longer, and we have to understand that external market pressures and idle capacity require companies to differentiate themselves and offer choices to the consumer. Companies have to live with product proliferation in today's marketplace and strategically realign or redesign their products and other business processes to meet these external pressures. Management must thoroughly understand strategies, both short- and long-term, on markets, products, processes, and distribution before embarking on an ambitious BPR project. Link strategies, core business processes, and critical success factors to local processes, focusing on performance improvement.

Absence of Top Management Commitment and Sustained Support

In a large organization, innovative ideas are often implemented in smaller plants or divisions. Depending on the culture of such enterprises, the larger hierarchy may not rapidly accept such ideas. Often an isolated business unit or plant implements a BPR study to enhance productivity without communicating with its corporate "think tank" staffers and executives. Such BPR initiatives will not succeed.

Political struggles arise out of BPR studies when the results are used to fix transfer prices among various entities. This is a classic dilemma in many corporations, in which corporate policy dictates that internal plants or divisions be used as the main sources (vertical integration). This does not encourage third-party sourcing to compete with internal producers. One large electrical equipment manufacturer's divisions sourced 100 percent of their parts from other divisions, always arguing in management meetings that they could be very competitive if only they were allowed to source from outside the corporation. Transfer pricing across divisions is by far the most controversial issue in the area of profitability today. BPR-based transfer pricing will work only if the entire enterprise is on the BPR bandwagon. This requires total commitment and support of the BPR concepts from top management. Also, under BPR, certain profitable products are shown to be unprofitable and vice versa. The person enjoying "unreasonable profit" will be a barrier to change.

Undefined Scope, Goals, and Objectives

Over the last several decades, there have been hundreds of management fads, quick fixes, and instant and easy cures for what happened to be wrong with business at the time. But BPR, when implemented properly, is not a fad but a totally new way of running a business, and a journey that is essential for survival in this very tough business climate. Yet, too often, we find companies are implementing BPR as if it were just another fad.

One mistake senior executives make is failing to fully and accurately define measurable performance requirements for market leadership or financial results for the company before implementing BPR. When no such measurable performance requirements have been identified, we normally see uncoordinated activities led by the finance, manufacturing, or marketing staff. These activities often have no clear purpose, no unifying direction, and no linkage to the strategic goals of the business unit.

It is thus very critical for the BPR team and the senior executives to spend considerable time initially brainstorming various broad issues: Do we need BPR? Can BPR address our problems? What do we want to get out of our BPR study? When and who should do it? What should be our short- and long-term goals with respect to BPR? Is it going to be a one-shot deal or a continuing journey? Goals, scope, and objectives for the BPR study should be clear right from the beginning. For example, typical goals might be to analyze processes and their performance, compute and trace product and customer costs to resources, analyze cost and revenue drivers, set up performance measurement metrics, and identify opportunities for continuous improvement. Without such specific objectives, BPR is bound to fail.

5

Failing to Train the Team Members

The past few years have seen an explosion in the number of consultants and institutions offering training classes for BPR implementation. Most of these classes don't add value, but not because they are poorly designed or delivered. Rather, most of them are conducted for the sake of training. The assumption is that sending people to BPR training is enough, that they will absorb some new skills and then apply them on their own back on the job. But these expectations rarely become a reality. Most companies believe that a handful of team members trained in BPR concepts and mock exercises (interviewing techniques, hardware and software training) will suffice for a successful BPR implementation.

Again, successfully interpreting the BPR results takes a deeper understanding of the strategic positioning of your products and services in the marketplace (market share, product lineup, pricing, process, design and logistics, capacity, leverage) as well as your sustainable core competencies (things you are very good at). Companies should take action based on the BPR results. With anything short of this, BPR will be yet another sophisticated business initiative with no relevance to strategy whatsoever. Also, if BPR is left with one process owner, it will be another nonfunctional system. Make sure a process-oriented cross-functional management system is in charge of the BPR project. Also, focus not only on cost reduction but on growth or growing the top-line profitability.

Relying on Complex Software and External Consultants

One of the problems with BPR is that it is such a broad new concept that almost anything management does can be classified as BPR. As with any new business opportunity, several consulting houses have repackaged their traditional productivity practices as BPR practices. The number of software packages in the marketplace is growing exponentially. Some come bundled with consulting services as well. Most of these software packages are nothing but simple databases or spreadsheets. Our opinion is that BPR software is not critical for a successful reengineering implementation. Unnecessary complexity in the software adds an extra variable to the learning curve. "Keep it splendidly simple" should be the attitude when it comes to tools. The software, if any, should be tailor-made to your needs.

We have also noticed that in an effort to accelerate learning and acquire expertise, many companies have brought in outside consultants. Consultants frequently provide canned solutions. Often, it takes a long time for them to understand the strategic nature of the company's business, its specifics and peculiarities. By the time the consultants begin to get a feel for their client's business, it is time for them to move on to the next assignment. The problem is not hiring consultants; it is entrusting the entire project to them without any team approach or participation from the company itself. Our recommendation is to hire consultants for the best training, practices, and advisory roles, not for actual implementation or decision making. Make sure that their role is to transfer technology to the BPR implementation team in a quick and orderly fashion. Ownership of the BPR system should rest with the company.

Not Empowering Team Members

Companies that are reengineering often do not empower the BPR team members. Many companies make BPR a manufacturing process exercise. Cross-functional teams often have members who are not high enough in the corporate hierarchy. Frequently the members are assigned to the BPR team not because of their high potential and good understanding of the business but because they had some extra time or were between projects. Committing the best members to the team is essential for success. During the implementation process, the members should be empowered (via announcements throughout the company) to access any details they need pertaining to the BPR project with no cross-boundary restrictions. How often does an organization let an inventory control person walk into the marketing office and start asking questions about quotes, orders, advertisements, or marketing strategy? Such open cross-boundary communication is an essential element of the BPR process. Also, anything less than 100 percent participation in the project is zero participation.

Once BPR is in place, many opportunities for continuous improvements will be identified. The team members must be empowered to select from all of the continuous improvement projects to determine which projects should be undertaken and by whom. Also, they must decide when to redesign and when to improve. These are alternative processes. The biggest failure is to treat BPR as a project and dissolve the team as soon as the project is over. When you create a team that is cross-functional with regard to its implementation, strategy, accountability, and time frame, you have pulled together a group of individuals who are probably the most knowledgeable in your company about many facets of your business. It is unwise and unprofitable to let that knowledge go to waste. Celebrating the project with a pizza party and dismantling the team is dumping resources and talent down the drain.

Focusing on Changing Culture versus Behavior

One of the most common mistakes companies make in implementing BPR is to focus on changing the culture without ever getting to the specifics of changing behavior. Most executives and senior managers understand the concepts of BPR, continuous improvement, performance measurement, or strategic management, but do not understand what they mean in terms of behavior or what they would mean to the organization in terms of change in culture.

Specifically defining these words makes them clear and measurable. For example, it is one thing to say that during the BPR study, employees will be working in cross-functional teams to define performance measurements or embark on continuous improvement programs. It is another to say, "The company will form a cross-functional team of employees from accounting, finance, engineering, marketing, and manufacturing. These members will meet every Monday morning; they will be empowered to make decisions, not just conduct studies, write reports, and submit a list of recommended actions to the CFO or the CEO and move back to their old jobs. Members will be recognized for their contributions, and their decisions will be supported. The team members will use structured problem-solving techniques such as brainstorming, consensus decision making, and Pareto analysis to analyze problems and develop action plans to improve overall performance."

Although in the long run companies must change their culture, they can do this only gradually through modifications in individual and team behavior.

Focusing on Short-Term Breakthroughs
Rather than Long-Term Process Improvements

Most executives seem to have a sense of urgency about fundamentally changing the way they run their businesses. Call it the BPR revolution or just plain survival under ever-mounting global pressures. Competition is increasing, and the strategies are complex. There is a squeeze on profits and rapid consolidation among homogeneous businesses, yet everyone wants to maintain their identity and independence and be a survivor in this ruthless marketplace.

We believe BPR is an approach to managing a business that, when implemented properly, should yield significant, long-term, continuous performance improvements. Expect a gradual, continuous improvement over time as decisions from the BPR team are put in motion, even with occasional setbacks. That said, companies do need some immediate improvements to generate interest in and gain support for long-term process improvements.

Most companies that have used BPR were or are in some sort of trouble—they are either unprofitable or losing market share. They looked at BPR as the "wonder drug" arriving from a prestigious business school or consulting firm. In reality, reengineering is not a cost-cutting exercise but a diagnostic tool to open up long-term opportunities. In other words, if you need to cut a few million dollars out of your operating costs in the next six months, BPR is not the answer. Instead, you will probably have to close plants, lay off workers, eliminate product lines, and do all the traditional things to get those savings. Once you have made and executed those tough decisions, then turn to BPR for the future. BPR is a journey, and the project needs to continue to integrate and coordinate all avenues of management, constantly striving to eliminate non-value-added activities.

Boyett and Conn's observations (1996) about corporations' most common TQM mistakes hold true for BPR as well: "If you have a major heart condition and need by-pass surgery to survive, dieting and exercise is not the answer. First get the surgery, then start changing your lifestyle so you can avoid more heart surgery or death in the future." BPR is a lifestyle change. It won't help you if you are on death's doorstep, but it is necessary for your long-term survival.

6

Where Do We Go from Here?

It should be clear from our discussion that the reengineering results have been mixed. Reengineering represents a significant investment as well as a significant challenge. Do not underestimate the difficulty and intensity of undergoing the process. It requires Herculean effort and strong conviction. Reengineering manuals should carry the disclaimer "Do not attempt without expertise and commitment; the probability of failure is significant, with disastrous results."

With that said, it would seem obvious that no single magic formula exists for reengineering success. Our "Do's and Don'ts" provide direction, but the action must come from a committed team with a full understanding of the strategic implications, knowledge of the core process, and awareness of the critical business issues. Again and again, the cases demonstrated that if there is a key to reengineering, it is the people.

Remember to start any reengineering initiative with a clear strategy. Too often reengineering manuals ignore that need. The choice of strategy must fit with the organization's own core competencies and the customer's perception of value. It is important to have this focus. The strategy acts as a sensitive, forward-looking antenna that receives signals from the future. It is an early warning system that allows quick adaptation to ever-changing conditions.

Today's consolidated corporation has begun to recognize the multiple dimensions along which it operates by forming strategic business units (SBUs). These SBUs will expand their role. Strategy will be based upon the SBUs. They will be more than a legal entity or end product or customer defined; each SBU will have the power to determine its own future direction.

As companies better understand the role and marketplace strategy of each SBU, they will naturally reconfigure to align themselves with their core business processes. As a result, the organizational chart will realign to cross-functional teams dictated by these critical business processes. From this we might expect companies to have a number of strategies targeted at different customer segments. This implies that the overarching, single strategic choice may be dead except within the one-dimensional business.

If an SBU defines its product/customer focus independently, then the resulting strategy will be much more targeted than that of the consolidated corporation. Moving the strategic decision making down into the organization allows for optimal matching of the value discipline (how the company will create value for its customer) and the choice of strategy. Upon examining a number of corporate strategies, Treacey and Wiersema (1996) identified the common value disciplines on which nearly all companies focus—customer intimacy, operational excellence, and product innovation. For example, companies that choose a strategy of customer intimacy as a way to create value would be competing on quality and customer retention. A choice of operational excellence would imply competing on cost. Product innovation implies competing on time. At the consolidated corporate level, the distinction between these dimensions is lost. Moving strategy development to the SBU level makes a sharp corporate focus possible. An SBU should choose one value discipline, or two at most, and become the top performer along the implied dimension. Whatever the SBU chooses, it should relentlessly pursue excellence.

Once the strategic choice is made, the critical/core business process is almost automatically identified. Too often reengineering projects get sidetracked by merely picking low-hanging fruit that is not mission critical. Guided by a well-understood strategy, reengineers should focus on the processes that generate the greatest value under that strategy. For example, take product innovation as a strategy. For most companies, excellence in research and development activities allows the organization to bring more novel products to market more quickly. They emphasize the money value of time instead of the more traditional business focus on the time value of money. In pursuing innovation, research and development becomes the critical/core business process, and improvement is measured by a reduction in development time. Innovative companies excel with their target customers—those who crave the latest development. On the other hand, customer intimacy might imply providing better quality in the service function. Operational excellence could result in lower costs through standardized manufacturing. Reengineering activities should focus on the appropriate competitive dimension and core process to support the chosen strategy/value discipline.

Intercompany Process Reengineering Is the Way to Go

Reengineering within the company was just the first stage of BPR. Corporate growth has reached a point where companies have begun to discuss ways of optimizing the processes between organizations. Reengineering has found its way into supply chain management. Companies have begun to take the reengineering methodology and apply it to processes extended outside the walls of their own business, processes that connect them to their suppliers and customers. Early results show that applying this intercompany reengineering to the entire supply-demand value chain magnifies and multiplies benefits (figure 14).

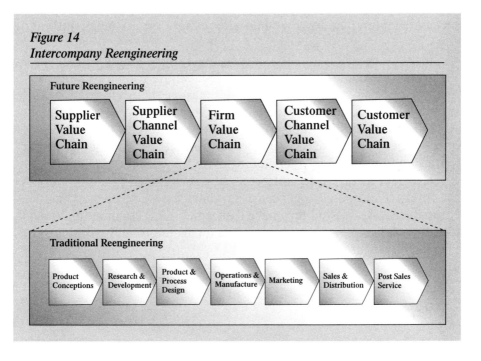

Figure 14
Intercompany Reengineering

Intercompany reengineering should be approached with an eye toward seeking nonlinear improvements. It is even more true that the architects of the new process need to think far outside the box. As the value chain gets longer, the degree to which the process can be altered or the amount of change that can take place also goes way up. No longer required to make stops at specified intervals along the way, the process can follow a very different path to arrive at the final destination.

The number and variety of parties represented in the value chain introduce new layers of complexity. At some point, every company in the supply chain might be a supplier or vendor, core customer, or end consumer, and in between are distributors, carriers, and various channels. Many companies currently count senior management committees as a key success factor for internal company reengineering. With so many parties involved, none of whom has the influence to force the others to consent, intercompany reengineering is sure to take longer, as it is based on consensus and cooperation. Parties must formulate a win-win strategy for all involved throughout the supply-demand value chain; successful intercompany reengineering cannot be a simple shifting of costs.

Technology is helping those attempting intercompany reengineering to overcome some of its complexity and facilitate cooperation. Companies are forming strategic alliances to measure the performance of the supply chain and are working to make it more transparent to all involved. The improved access to information allows costs to be taken out of the process, because companies are eliminating non-value-added activities and redundancies, shortening cycle times, and reducing errors.

The next direction for intercompany reengineering is the Web. As the Internet continues to generate new businesses and business models, companies will use what they have learned about reengineering to move into the realm of electronic commerce or to improve the online products they have already developed.

Reengineering for Growth

The word "reengineering" conjures up painful memories of the recession of the late eighties and early nineties. People remember massive downsizing, horrible layoffs, and agonizing outsourcing. These actions represented corporations' best attempts at cost reduction. For many, reengineering will always be a method for reducing costs and an unpleasant one at that.

It is clear, however, that reengineering has other applications, too. Reengineering can be applied to dramatically change the business as a response to growth conditions. Universal Financial Corporation demonstrates that reengineering principles can be used to develop a new process that will capture an even greater share of the market. More and more, companies are using reengineering to grow their business—to introduce new products, provide better service, and become more responsive to their customers. It used to be that the focus of a reengineering project was inward, on slimming the organization. Companies are beginning to recognize the value of reengineering with a focus on the customer, to fatten their revenue.

Companies are measuring reengineering benefits less in terms of cost savings and more in terms of sales growth. Reengineering works on both the expense line items and the top line. The result can be a twice-blessed bottom line.

Reengineering—A Mechanism for Change

Reengineering will never become easy, because it represents a break with the past, a quantum leap in a new direction. What do you prefer when you wake up in the morning? Softly played instrumental jazz that allows you to gradually slip from your slumber, or a bucket of ice-cold water tossed on you to jolt you out of bed? Reengineering is the bucket of cold water. No wonder it has something of a tainted reputation.

Many corporations were asleep at the wheel. The thumping of competition, the loud complaints of their customers, the noise of a changing marketplace could not wake them up. It was almost too late when the reengineering bucket came along. It sure hurts to have to wake up that way.

Some companies have learned their lesson. They no longer need reengineering to react to shifts in their environment. They recognize the perpetual nature of change and have become flexible, dynamic organizations that anticipate movements in the market. These companies are constantly tuning their operations and reinforcing the fit with their customers' expectations. For these companies, change is a way of life.

Others find change much harder. They adopt a new strategy and a new vision and fundamentally shift their business, but they are not experimenting and scanning their environment. They change the steps in the process as a result of reengineering, but they expect the new process to remain in place for the next 30 years. For certain corporate cultures, change will never be a continuous, evolving proposition. Change comes in large strides, in comprehensive shifts in direction led by top management.

For such companies or for companies that find themselves in circumstances that call for large-scale change, reengineering makes sense. Reengineering is a valid approach for implementing sweeping corporate reform, but there are alternatives. Companies can take a more proactive approach and view change as a continuous process. Such companies will constantly modify their operations to better meet the dynamic needs of the marketplace. For today's companies, change is no longer a one-time reengineering project but an everyday fact of life.

A P P E N D I X   A

Survey

Financial Executives Research Foundation, Inc.
Business Process Reengineering Research Project
Fax/Mail Survey

Please use additional pages if necessary
(Underlined terms are defined at the end of this survey.)

Please provide us with the following information about you and your company:

Name _____

Title _____

Company _____

Address _____

Telephone Number _____ Fax _____

Part I—Situation Prior to
Business Process Reengineering (BPR)

1. **What situation created the need for reengineering?** (Please check all that apply)

High cost/inefficient performance of processes ☐
Declining margins ☐
Declining market share for product lines ☐
Lower stock price compared to industry ☐
Desire to focus on fewer products/processes ☐
Higher defect rate in products ☐
Lower customer satisfaction ☐
Other _____ ☐

2. **How long did the situation last that created the need for BPR?** (Please check one)

6 months – 1 year ☐
1 year – 2 years ☐
More than 2 years ☐
Other _____ ☐

3. **What other alternatives were considered instead of BPR?** (Please check all that apply)

Economic value added ☐
Efficient consumer response ☐
Corporate restructuring (e.g., spinoffs) ☐
Outsourcing ☐
Different employee incentive schemes ☐
Other (please describe) _____ ☐

4. **Why were other alternatives rejected?** (Please check all that apply)

Higher cost ☐
Likely negative effect on employee morale ☐
Lack of internal expertise for implementation ☐
Difficulties in implementation ☐
Other (please describe) _____ ☐

Part II—During and After
Business Process Reengineering (BPR)

5. **When did the BPR program begin?**

Year _____ Month _____

6. **When did the BPR program end?**

Year _____ Month _____ It is still in effect. ☐

7. **What functional areas/processes were reengineered?** (Please check all that apply)

Procurement and Inventory Control
Procurement ☐
Warehouse ☐
Inventory ☐

Supply chain ☐
Accounts payable ☐

Manufacturing
Raw material delivery ☐
Manufacturing ☐
Quality control ☐

Sales
Order delivery ☐
Accounts receivable/collection ☐

Customer Service
Customer service ☐
Warranty ☐
Other (please describe) _____ ☐

8. **How was the reengineering accomplished?** (Please check all that apply)
Centralization of processes ☐
Decentralization of processes ☐
Computerization of processes ☐
Specialization of processes ☐
Other (please describe) _____ ☐

9. **Of the total hours spent on the BPR program implementation, what percentage of time was spent by in-house personnel and what percentage was spent by outside consultants?**

In-house personnel _____ %
Outside consultants _____ %
Total 100%
Information not available ☐

10. **Why were outside consultants employed in the program?** (Please check all that apply)
Less expensive ☐
Expertise in the area ☐
Need for fresh thinking about the process ☐
Prior relationships with consultants ☐
Competitors in the industry use the same consultant ☐

Validate and provide credibility for internal efforts ☐

Other (please describe) _____ ☐

11. **What was the cumulative cost of in-house personnel and consultants involved in the implementation of the BPR program?** ($ thousands)

In-house personnel ____

Outside consultants ____

Total ____

Cost details not available ☐

12. **What, if any, degree of disruption occurred in the workplace during the implementation of the BPR program?**

1	2	3	4	5
☐	☐	☐	☐	☐
No disruption				Major disruption

13. **What was the effect on employee morale during the implementation of the BPR program?**

1	2	3	4	5
☐	☐	☐	☐	☐
Very positive				Very negative

14. **Please provide possible reasons for high or low morale (e.g., employees were involved in the BPR program and this resulted in high morale).**

15. **What assurances were provided by management regarding employees' job situation?** (Please check all that apply)

No guarantee ☐

A guarantee of no layoffs ☐

Possible relocation to other business units or segments ☐

A guaranteed job fair ☐

Severance pay in case of layoff ☐

Other (please describe) _____ ☐

16. How much, if any, organizational restructuring occurred as a result of the BPR program?

1	2	3	4	5
☐	☐	☐	☐	☐

No Restructuring   Major Restructuring

17. What changes in the compensation structure and performance evaluation took place as a result of the BPR program?

No change in the compensation structure ☐
Minor changes in the compensation structure ☐
Significant changes in the compensation structure ☐
If you checked "significant changes," please explain.

18. Were the goals set out to address the identified problems accomplished through the BPR program?

Yes, benefits exceeded cost ☐
Yes, benefits equaled cost ☐
No, benefits **did not** exceed cost ☐
Difficult to evaluate ☐
Other ☐
Please explain your response.

19. How did you account for BPR program costs in your financial statements?

Costs were expensed and treated as extraordinary items ☐
Costs were expensed as ordinary expenses ☐
Costs were capitalized and are being amortized
    over ____ years. ☐
Other (please describe) _____ ☐

20. Any other comments that you wish to add regarding the initiation, implementation, and evaluation of BPR.

Glossary of Underlined Terms

Business Process Reengineering (BPR)

A fundamental rethinking and radical redesign of business processes to achieve dramatic improvements in critical, contemporary measures of performance, such as cost, quality, service, and speed.

Economic Value Added

The residual income left over from operating profit after the cost of capital has been subtracted. It is calculated as the earnings before interest less a capital charge on total capital (debt plus equity).

Efficient Consumer Response

A strategy in which the manufacturer, distributor, and retailer study methods to work closely together, in order to eliminate excess costs from the supply chain and better serve the consumer.

Job Fair

A meeting arranged by the employer for the potentially displaced workers to help them obtain employment elsewhere.

Interview Protocol

I. Need for Business Process Reengineering

1. How would you describe your company's reengineering program?
   A. Reactive
   B. Proactive
   C. Strategic
   D. Other

2. What was the operational and financial position of the company when the reengineering program was initiated?
   A. The company was in a sound operational and financial position.
   B. The company's operational and/or financial position needed strengthening.
   C. Other

3. What issues or problems (operational, financial, or customer) triggered the need for action?
   A. Loss of market share
   B. Excessive costs
   C. Falling stock price
   D. Other

4. What group first identified the issue or problem, or an aspect of the issue or problem?
   A. Senior management
   B. Middle management
   C. Other employees
   D. Consultants

5. How long after the issue or problem was first identified did management decide to reengineer the business process?

6. Why was reengineering used instead of other alternatives (e.g., spinoffs, outsourcing, or a different employee incentive scheme)?
   A. A "clean sheet" or "blue sky" approach was needed because the existing process was archaic.
   B. Top management preferred reengineering.
   C. Reengineering was suggested by outside consultants.
   D. Competing companies had used BPR.
   E. Technological changes made the old processes obsolete or less competitive.
   F. There was a change in market conditions.
   G. Other

II. Attributes of the Reengineering Effort

1. What were the critical success factors?

2. How were the critical success factors measured?
   A. Market share
   B. Operational efficiency
   C. Financial results
   D. Other

3. Were cross-functional areas (e.g., finance, IT, marketing, and operations) taken into consideration in selecting the processes to be reengineered? How were these factors addressed?

4. What were the budget constraints?
   A. Time
   B. Resources

5. Who was on the BPR team? What functions were represented? What levels of management were represented?

6. What was the time commitment of the BPR team?
   A. 100%
   B. Less than 100%

7. What was the consultant's role?
   A. No consultants were used.
   B. Consultants were used extensively.
   C. Consultants were used as coaches.

8. Was a pilot BPR program considered? If not, please explain.

9. What educational materials were developed for the affected employees?

10. Were other initiatives tried in conjunction with the BPR program (e.g., total quality management)?

III. Implementation, Project Management, and Evaluation

1. Was business process reengineering implemented at the corporate level or at the divisional level? Please explain.

2. What was the expected effect on day-to-day operations during implementation? How did the expected effort compare with actual results?

3. Who had the authority to change the reengineering program's direction?

4. Was the use of new information technology considered? Was the use of enterprise-wide software applications (e.g., Systems, Applications, and Products in Data Processing, or SAP), considered? Please explain.

5. What type of evaluation was used for the results?

6. How was the success of the BPR program measured?
   A. Customer satisfaction
   B. Operational efficiency
   C. Financial results
   D. Employee morale
   E. Other

7. What problems were anticipated before the implementation began? What crisis management plans were made?

8. What problems or crises were actually experienced?

9. What continuous improvement programs, if any, are now being used?

IV. Retrospective

1. If you were to implement the BPR program today, what would you do differently?

2. Is there anything that has not already been discussed that you would like to add?

APPENDIX C

References

Bleakley, Fred R. "Going for Growth: Many Firms See Gains of Cost-Cutting Over, Push to Lift Revenues." *Wall Street Journal,* Jul. 5, 1996, Sec. A, p. 1.

Boyett, J.H., and H.P. Conn. "What is wrong with TQM?" private communication, 1996.

Cooper, R. "You Need an ABC System When..." *Harvard Business Review*, Jan/Feb 1989.

Hammer, Michael. "Reengineering Work: Don't Automate, Obliterate." *Harvard Business Review,* Jul. 1990, pp. 104–112.

Hammer, Michael, and James Champy. *Reengineering the Corporation: A Manifesto for Business Revolution.* New York: HarperBusiness: A Division of Harper-Collins Publishers, 1993.

Hammer, Michael, with Steven A. Stanton. *The Reengineering Revolution.* New York: HarperBusiness, 1995.

Hogarty, D.B. "The Future of Middle Managers." *Management Review,* September 1993, pp. 51–53.

Karlgaard, Rich. "ASAP Interview: Mike Hammer." *Forbes Supplement,* September 13, 1993, pp. 69–75.

Improving Performance: How to Manage the White Space on the Organization Chart. San Francisco: Jossey-Bass, Inc., 1995.

Randall, Robert M. "The Reengineer." *Planning Review,* May 1, 1993.

State of Reengineering Report—Executive Summary. Cambridge, MA: 1994.

Strassmann, Paul A. "The Roots of Business Process Reengineering." *American Programmer,* June 1995.

Treacy, Michael, and Fred Wiersema. *The Discipline of Market Leaders: Choose Your Customers, Narrow Your Focus, Dominate Your Market.* Reading, MA: Addison-Wesley Publishing Company, 1995.

Bala V. Balachandran began his teaching career in 1960 as a graduate student at Annamalai University, India. In 1967 he moved to the University of Dayton and in 1971 to Carnegie-Mellon University, Pittsburgh, where he taught management courses while working on his doctorate. From 1979 to 1983 he chaired the Department of Accounting and Information Systems; in 1984 he was appointed Distinguished Professor of Accounting and Information Systems and Decision Sciences at the Kellogg Graduate School of Management. He is one of three Kellogg faculty members who started the Information Resource Management Program at Northwestern in 1974. He has authored more than 55 research articles and is currently writing a managerial accounting textbook with emphasis on cost management in an automated manufacturing environment. He is department editor in accounting for *Management Science,* associate editor for *The Accounting Review,* and on the editorial boards of *Contemporary Accounting Research* and *Journal of Accounting, Auditing and Finance.*

Professor Balachandran's research deals with performance evaluation, cost management, activity-based management, allocation models, and forecasting. His work has earned numerous scholastic honors, awards, and fellowships, and he serves as a consultant to senior management in industry, as well as to the U.S. Air Force. He has provided executive education for various companies and the government and is the program director for "Managing Cost Information for Effective Strategic Decisions," a three-day program conducted during the spring and fall each year at the James L. Allen Center.

S. Ramu Thiagarajan is currently quantitative research strategist at Mellon Capital Management Corporation in San Francisco. When doing the research for this study, he was an assistant professor of accounting in the Kellogg Graduate School of Management, Northwestern University and the Coopers & Lybrand Fellow of Accounting. He obtained his master's degree in accounting from the University of Illinois at Champaign Urbana and his Ph.D. in business administration from the University of Florida in 1989.

His research interests include the roles of both accounting and nonaccounting information in fundamental analysis. His scholarly papers have been published in major accounting/finance journals, such as *Journal of Accounting Research, Journal of Accounting and Economics, Journal of Accounting, Auditing and Finance,* and the *Review of Accounting Studies.* His work has also been featured in *The Wall Street Journal* and *The Economist.* His current research interests are the role of short interest, the role of accounting information in IPOs, and the use of nonaccounting information in detecting management fraud.

Dr. Thiagarajan has received numerous honors and awards. In 1993 and 1994 he and his coauthor received research grants from the Banking Research Center in Kellogg and Deloitte and Touche for their ongoing work on the role of financial and nonfinancial information in detecting management fraud. He was awarded the first Sidney J. Levy teaching award for an untenured assistant professor, voted for by the faculty of Kellogg, in 1993.

Prior to entering academic life, Dr. Thiagarajan spent three years auditing large corporations in India and working for a year as a management accountant for Hindustan Lever Limited in India.

ACKNOWLEDGMENTS

We would like to thank Harry Kraemer of Baxter International for meeting with us on two different occasions, for his passion for the project, and for writing the foreword. We would like to thank all the participants to the case studies—in particular, Norman Thompson of American Express; the team from IBM, which made an impressive presentation for us at Kellogg, including Marc Slocum, John Kirby, Mark Grace, Paul Mugge, John Patterson, and Brian Balthazard; and the officials from Universal Financial Corporation, Midwest Utility, and Pfizer, all of whom provided their valuable time through meetings and telephone calls. We would also like to thank all the participants in our two surveys, who are too many to name individually but very important for our analysis.

We would like to thank Scott Reader for helping us with the cases and organizing the monograph, and Kathleen Reader for patiently reading and editing it. Also, we appreciate Vikram Krishnan's assistance in the presentation of the survey findings in chapter 2. The authors acknowledge Ning Tang for his contributions at the beginning of the project and Qi Lu for his input on the analysis of the survey findings.

We would like to thank the staff of the Accounting and Information Systems department, Bonnie Lee, Marlene Ruby, and Joan Palmer, for being patient with all our requests throughout this project.

The grant that made this project possible came from the Financial Executives Research Foundation. The time and commitment of Bill Sinnett, Jim Lewis, and Camille Guérin were the key ingredients in making this project successful.